EXPERIENCING THE JEWISH HOLIDAYS

JOEL LURIE GRISHAVER

TORAH AURA PRODUCTIONS

ISBN 10: 1-934527-43-2

ISBN 13: 978-1-934527-43-6

Photo credits: Gustavo Andrade, page 13 (middle); Noam Armonn, page 5 (bottom); AVTG, pages 76, 77; David Bleicher, pages 63, 64, 65, 87, 98; Boohoo, page 12 (bottom); Aron, Brand, page 111; Liudmila Chernova, page 41; Odelia Cohen, page 92; Gil Cohen Magen/Reuters/Corbis, pages 112–113; Comstock, pages 96–97; Paul Cowan, page 71; Chaim Danzinger, page 42; Dblight, page 7; Terric Delayn, page 16; Frank Dixon, pages 125–127; Alesander Dvorak, page 73; Elena Elisseeva, pages 22 (right), 117; Fuse, page 49; Daniel Gonzales, page 68; Alex Gui, page 101; Zlatko Guzmic, page 80; Haya-p, page 12 (top); Kurt Holter, page 9; Imagebybarbara, pages 30–31; Imagesource, page 14; Alexander Ishchenko, page 23 (right); Israel Ministry of Tourism, page 123; Evgeniy Ivanov, page 13 (top); JCEIV, page 110; Dorling Kidersley, page 25; Arkandiusz Komski, page 48; Robert Lam, page 94; Marcin-linfernum, page 22 (left); Gregory Markov, page 8 (top); Carmen Martinez Banús, pages 74–75, 83; Mordechai Meiri, pages 10–11, 89; Ekaterina Monakhova, page 56 (right); Ethan Myerson, cover, pages 38, 56 (left); Aleksey Oleynikov, pages 118–119; Laurie Patterson, page 70; Pavelr28, page 54; Catalin Petolea, page 122; Pink-cotton-candy, page 46; S1001, page 23 (left); John Said, page 6; David Schrader, page 40; Elzbieta Selowska, page 105; Skirball Museum Archives, pages 86, 88; James L. Stanfield/National Geographic, page 20; Sterling-photo, page 102; Konstantin Sutyagin, page 81; Tova Teitelbaum, pages 4–5, 44, 66; Trinacria, page 116; Christine Tripp, pages 17 (top), 104, 106; Martin Trommer, pages 108–109; Webking, page 69; Terry Wilson, page 72; Wrangle, page 124; Zentilia, page 32; Kenneth C. Zirkel, pages 60–61. Most of the images in this book come from the following online stock houses: CorbisImages, Fotalia, Getty Images, IStockphoto and Shutterstock. Thank you to Yair Emanuel for the use of his Havdalah set on page 58.

Torah Aura Productions • 4423 Fruitland Avenue, Los Angeles, CA 90058
(800) BE-Torah • (800) 238-6724 • (323) 585-7312 • fax (323) 585-0327
E-MAIL <misrad@torahaura.com> • Visit the Torah Aura website at www.torahaura.com
Manufactured in Malaysia

TABLE OF CONTENTS

ROSH HA-SHANAH
AND YOM KIPPUR

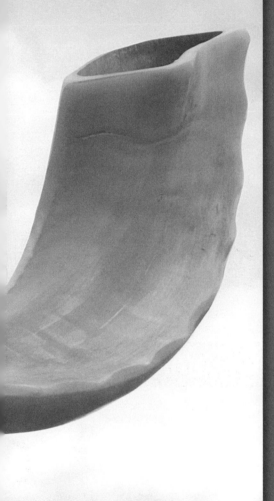

ROSH HA-SHANAH

OPPORTUNITIES

○ Greeting your class with *"L'Shanah Tovah"*.

○ Eating apples/ḥallah and honey with the *brakhah*.

○ Blowing the shofar.

○ Making a Rosh ha-Shanah card.

FAMILY OPPORTUNITIES

○ Sending out Rosh ha-Shanah cards.

○ Lighting the candles, saying the Kiddush, and blessing a round ḥallah to welcome Rosh ha-Shanah.

○ Going to Rosh ha-Shanah services.

YOM KIPPUR

OPPORTUNITIES

○ Practicing saying "I'm Sorry".

○ Making an Al Ḥet List.

FAMILY OPPORTUNITIES

○ Saying "I'm Sorry" to each other.

○ Fasting part of the day.

○ Lighting Yizkor candles.

○ Going to Yom Kippur services.

Beginning the Year

The Jewish year begins twice. The Jewish calendar begins in the spring, but Rosh ha-Shanah, the Jewish New Year, is in the fall. Rosh ha-Shanah is the first of the Hebrew month of *Tishrei*. Rosh ha-Shanah and the days that follow are called the Ten Days of Repentance. They are designed to help you become the best possible you. The tenth day is Yom Kippur, the Day of Atonement.

The Hebrew month before Rosh ha-Shanah is called *Elul*. All of Elul is devoted to getting your heart and mind ready for Rosh ha-Shanah.

REFLECTION QUESTION

One way I can get my heart and mind ready for Rosh ha-Shanah is

_____

_____

_____

_____.

לְשָׁנָה טוֹבָה L'Shanah Tovah

רֹאשׁ *Rosh* means "head" or "start." שָׁנָה *Shanah* means "year."
טוֹב *Tov* means "good." On Rosh ha-Shanah we greet each other with
לְשָׁנָה טוֹבָה *L'Shanah Tovah*—"Have a good year."

Shake hands with everyone in your class and greet them *"L'Shanah Tovah."*

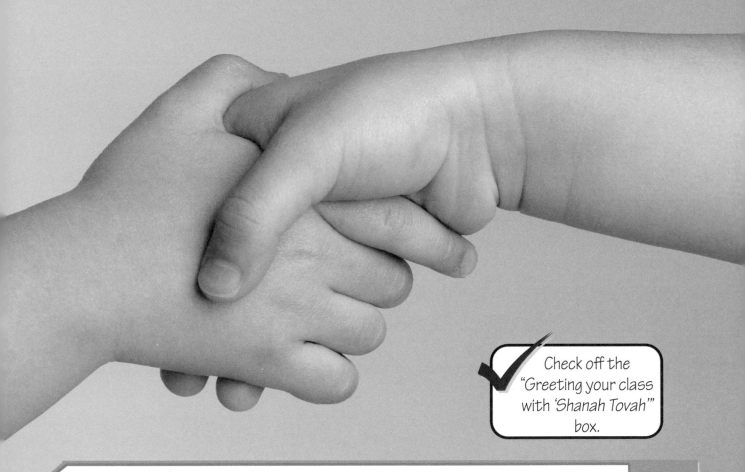

✓ Check off the "Greeting your class with 'Shanah Tovah'" box.

What would have to happen for your new year to be the best? _____

_____

_____

REFLECTION QUESTION

7

Rosh ha-Shanah Food

Four foods help us welcome Rosh ha-Shanah.

רִמּוֹן

Pomegranate

The pomegranate is called a *rimon* in Hebrew. The pomegranate is said to have 613 seeds that remind us of the 613 *mitzvot* (commandments) in the Torah. A pomegranate is also a symbol of a fruitful new year.

Honey and Apples

Honey is sweet. We eat it on Rosh ha-Shanah as a wish for a sweet new year. When we dip apples in it we say:

בָּרוּךְ אַתָּה יי אֱלֹהֵינוּ מֶלֶךְ הָעוֹלָם
בּוֹרֵא פְּרִי הָעֵץ.

Barukh Attah Adonai, Eloheinu, Melekh ha-Olam, Borei Pri ha-Etz.

Praised are You, Eternal, our God, Ruler of the Cosmos, Who creates the fruit of the tree.

דְּבַשׁ

תַּפּוּחַ

Hallah

חַלָּה

חַלָּה *Hallah* is the braided egg bread Jews eat on Shabbat and holidays. On Rosh ha-Shanah we use a special round ḥallah. The roundness reminds us that the year goes in a circle, too. Rosh ha-Shanah is the beginning of the circle. It is a custom to dip the Rosh ha-Shanah ḥallah in honey. When we eat ḥallah and honey we say:

בָּרוּךְ אַתָּה יי אֱלֹהֵינוּ מֶלֶךְ הָעוֹלָם הַמּוֹצִיא לֶחֶם מִן הָאָרֶץ.

Barukh Attah Adonai, Eloheinu, Melekh ha-Olam, ha-Motzi Leḥem min ha-Aretz.

Praised are You, Eternal, our God, Ruler of the Cosmos, Who brings forth bread from the earth.

REFLECTION QUESTION

What is the sweetest thing in your life?

_____

_____

_____

When you *dip* apples (and/or) ḥallah in honey and say the *brakhah*, check off the "Eat Apples/Ḥallah and Honey with a *brakhah*" box.

Hearing the Shofar

The voice of the *shofar* is the voice of Rosh ha-Shanah. The shofar is a ram's horn that has been turned into a musical instrument. It makes a sharp, piercing, sound. In ancient times the shofar was used to call the people together. On Rosh ha-Shanah we use the shofar to wake up our souls.

The shofar makes four calls:

Teki'ah is one long call.

Shevarim is three notes put together.

Teru'ah is nine quick notes.

Teki'ah Gedolah is a really long call that comes at the end.

שׁוֹפָר

Maimonides, a famous Jewish philosopher and physician, wrote:

The shofar says: "Awake, sleepers, from your sleep! Arise, slumberers, from your slumber! Look at your deeds. Return in repentance. Remember your Creator!"

(Hilkhot Teshuvah, chapter 3)

REFLECTION QUESTION

How can a soul be asleep? How does one wake up a soul?_____

_____

_____

10

בָּרוּךְ אַתָּה יי אֱלֹהֵינוּ מֶלֶךְ הָעוֹלָם
אֲשֶׁר קִדְּשָׁנוּ בְּמִצְוֹתָיו וְצִוָּנוּ לִשְׁמֹעַ קוֹל שׁוֹפָר.

Barukh Attah Adonai, Eloheinu Melekh ha-Olam, asher kid'shanu b'mitzvotav, v'tzivanu li'shmo'a kol shofar.

Praised are You, Eternal our God, Ruler of the Cosmos, Who makes us holy with the commandments and has commanded us to hear the voice of the shofar.

Here is a photograph of me trying to blow the shofar.

I was ☐ good   ☐ not so good   ☐ terrible
at sounding the shofar.

✓ When you've heard the shofar, check off the "Hearing the Shofar" box.

To me the shofar sounds like _____

_____

The shofar said to me, " _____

_____ "

REFLECTION QUESTION

11

Rosh ha-Shanah Cards

It is a custom to send Rosh ha-Shanah cards to family and friends. Make a card to send.

Decorate it with a shofar, apples and honey, a round ḥallah, a pomegranate, or the Hebrew or English greeting "*L'shanah Tovah*." Think about what other Jewish images you could use.

Shofar שׁוֹפָר

Hebrew greeting לְשָׁנָה טוֹבָה

L'Shanah Tovah

English greeting

תַּפּוּחַ

apple

דְּבַשׁ

honey

pomegranate

רִמּוֹן

What is the thing I most wish for everyone in the coming year? _____

_____

_____

_____ .

Here is a photograph of my Rosh ha-Shanah card.

✓ Check off the "making a Rosh ha-Shanah card" box.

T'shuvah: Turning Things Around

The ten days from Rosh ha-Shanah to Yom Kippur are called the עֲשֶׂרֶת יְמֵי תְּשׁוּבָה *Eseret Y'mei T'shuvah* (The Ten Days of Repentance). תְּשׁוּבָה *T'shuvah* (repentance) really means "to turn things around." During the *Eseret Y'mei T'shuvah* we look at our behavior. We find the things we can do better. We make a commitment to change. We turn our lives around.

Four Steps to Repentance

Rabbi Isaac Arama taught: There are four steps to repentance.
1. Admitting that you have done wrong.
2. Saying you are sorry.
3. Fixing what you broke or hurt.
4. Doing the work needed to change so that you never repeat the same mistake.

Doing these four steps is "turning things around."

Work out a movement for each of the four steps. Turn the four movements into a dance.

14

Practicing "I Am Sorry"

One of the hardest parts of doing t'shuvah is admitting that you are wrong and then saying, "I am sorry." On this page we are going to practice being wrong.

Pick a partner and act out the first two situations. Then change partners and do it again with situations three and four. Finally, find a third partner and act out the last two situations.

1. You are a child who is playing on the computer. Three times your parent asks you to stop, and you say, "Give me a minute." The fourth time your parent asks, you yell at him or her. Now it is your turn to say, "I am sorry."

2. There is a child in your school to whom everyone is mean. You are mean, too. Now it is time for you to say, "I am sorry" for the way you acted.

3. You are a parent. You yell at your child for breaking something. You learn that someone else broke the thing. Now you have to say, "I am sorry."

4. You have a friend who has been a friend for a long time. A new kid comes to school. You completely ignore your old friend to make a new one. Now you realize that it is time to say, "I'm sorry."

5. You cheat and fool your teacher. You get an "A." A show on TV convinces you that it is better to be honest. You decide that you now have to tell the truth and say, "I am sorry."

6. Make up a case of your own.

After acting out these stories, check off your "practicing saying I'm sorry" box.

REFLECTION QUESTION

The hardest part of saying I'm sorry is_____

_____

_____

_____

Yom Kippur

Yom Kippur is a long day. *Erev Yom Kippur* is the evening when Yom Kippur starts. We have a last meal before sunset, and then adults begin to fast. Not eating helps us think about our behavior. At evenings services there is an important prayer called *Kol Nidrei*. It talks about promises that we made that we did not keep.

On the day of Yom Kippur there are services almost all day long. We work on changing from the way we have done wrong and promise to be better in the coming year. One important prayer is called עַל חֵטְא *Al Het* (for the sins). חֵטְא *Het* means "arrow." The Jewish idea of doing wrong is "missing the mark." It is like shooting at the target and not hitting the bull's-eye. Yom Kippur helps us to aim better.

עַל חֵטְא Al <u>H</u>et

During the *Al <u>H</u>et* we hit our chest over our heart for each way we may have missed the mark.

Here are three sentences from the traditional *Al <u>H</u>et*. Read and discuss them. Write one of your own. Then assemble a class list.

We have missed the mark by mean speaking.
And we have missed the mark by sneaky actions.

We have missed the mark by not acting the way God wants.
And we have missed the mark by the way we judge.

We have missed the mark by things we did on purpose and by accident.
And we have missed the mark by not showing respect to parents and teachers.

We have missed the mark by _____

_____ .

And we have missed the mark by _____

_____ .

וְעַל כֻּלָּם אֱלוֹהַּ סְלִיחוֹת. סְלַח לָנוּ. מְחַל לָנוּ. כַּפֶּר לָנוּ:

V'al kulam Eloha s'li<u>h</u>ot. S'la<u>h</u> la-nu. M'<u>h</u>al la-nu. Kaper la-nu.

For all of these, God of forgiveness, forgive us, pardon us, grant us atonement.

 Check off your "*Al Het* list" box.

SUKKOT

SUKKOT OPPORTUNITIES

○ Dwelling in a sukkah and saying the brakhah.

○ Making a sukkah decoration.

○ Shaking the etrog and lulav and saying the brakhah.

○ Explaining the etrog and lulav.

○ Ushpizin, inviting Jews from the past into the sukkah.

FAMILY OPPORTUNITIES

○ Building a sukkah.

○ Sleeping in the sukkah.

○ Going to Sukkot services.

○ Reading part of the Book of Ecclesiastes.

○ Celebrating *Hosha'nah Rabbah*.

○ Celebrating *Shmini Atzeret*.

The Sukkah

A sukkah is a temporary hut or booth that is built just for Sukkot. The words of the sukkah *brakhah* (blessing) tell us what to do.

בָּרוּךְ אַתָּה יי אֱלֹהֵינוּ מֶלֶךְ הָעוֹלָם
אֲשֶׁר קִדְּשָׁנוּ בְּמִצְוֹתָיו וְצִוָּנוּ לֵישֵׁב בַּסֻּכָּה.

Barukh Attah Adonai Eloheinu Melekh ha-Olam Asher Kidshanu b'Mitzvotav
v'Tzivanu Leishev ba-Sukkah.

Praised are You Eternal Our God, Ruler of the Cosmos, Who made us Holy through the mitzvot and made it a mitzvah for us to dwell/sit in the sukkah.

This sukkah mitzvah comes from the phrase "לֵישֵׁב בַּסֻּכָּה *Leishev b'Sukkah*," which can be translated two ways. It is either "sit" in a sukkah or "live" in a sukkah.

Some Jews actually move furniture into the sukkah and live there. Some Jews just put a table and chairs in the sukkah and eat in there. Some Jews just go out to a sukkah and eat something (with a *brakhah*) and say the *brakhah*.

20

Dwelling in a Sukkah

If it is now Sukkot, go into the sukkah. Sit if you can. Eat if you can.

Here is a leaf or needle from our sukkah.

Say the *brakhah* and check off the opportunity of dwelling in a sukkah.

סֻכָּה

What did it feel like to be in the sukkah? _____

_____.

What did you think about in the sukkah? _____

_____.

Why? There are at least four different reasons why we dwell in the Sukkah.

1.

After we left Egypt and when we lived for forty years in the wilderness we lived in sukkot. The sukkah reminds us of our time in the wilderness.

2.

When we entered the Land of Israel we lived in sukkot when we harvested our fields. The sukkah reminds us that we were once farmers.

Art Project

Break your class into four groups. Have each group design a sukkah decoration for one of the four reasons we dwell in sukkot.

Here is a photograph of my group's decoration.

3.

When we lived in the Land of Israel we went up to Jerusalem three times a year. This was for Sukkot, Pesa<u>h</u> and Shavuot. When we visited Jerusalem many of us lived in sukkot. The sukkah reminds us of going up to Jerusalem.

4.

When we go into the sukkah in the fall, before the winter comes, we make a connection with the environment God created.

 Check off your "Make a sukkah decoration" opportunity.

Sukkah Rules

To build a sukkah, these are the major rules.

1. The sukkah must be large enough to fit a person's head, most of his or her body, and a table.

2. The walls of the sukkah can be made of any material. They have to be strong enough to stand up to an ordinary wind.

3. It is a custom to start building the sukkah right after Yom Kippur.

4. We cover the roof with the branches of trees or with reeds. They are not to be tied together. A sukkah roof cannot have nails or screws.

5. There should be enough branches on the roof so there is more shade than sun. You should be able to see the stars through the roof at night.

6. A sukkah built underneath the branches of a tree is not acceptable.

What do these rules teach you about the sukkah? ____

_____

_____

REFLECTION QUESTION

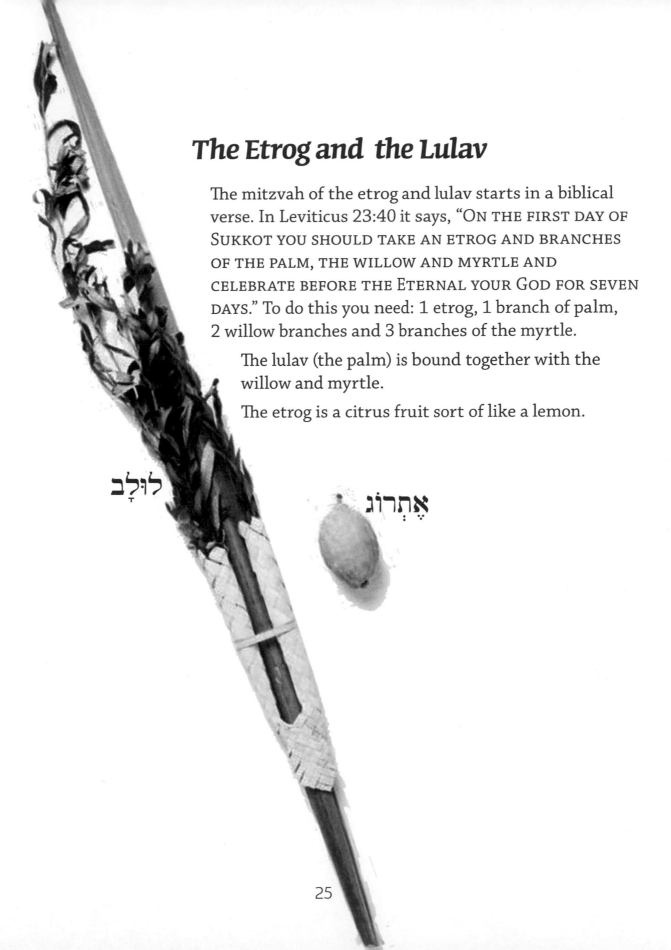

The Etrog and the Lulav

The mitzvah of the etrog and lulav starts in a biblical verse. In Leviticus 23:40 it says, "ON THE FIRST DAY OF SUKKOT YOU SHOULD TAKE AN ETROG AND BRANCHES OF THE PALM, THE WILLOW AND MYRTLE AND CELEBRATE BEFORE THE ETERNAL YOUR GOD FOR SEVEN DAYS." To do this you need: 1 etrog, 1 branch of palm, 2 willow branches and 3 branches of the myrtle.

The lulav (the palm) is bound together with the willow and myrtle.

The etrog is a citrus fruit sort of like a lemon.

לוּלָב

אֶתְרוֹג

How to Shake the Lulav

1. Face east. Hold the lulav in your right hand and the etrog in your left. Bring your hands together with the part of the etrog that was attached to the tree facing up.

2. Recite the blessing:

בָּרוּךְ אַתָּה יי אֱלֹהֵינוּ מֶלֶךְ הָעוֹלָם
אֲשֶׁר קִדְּשָׁנוּ בְּמִצְוֹתָיו וְצִוָּנוּ עַל נְטִילַת לוּלָב.

Barukh Attah Adonai Eloheinu Melekh ha-Olam Asher Kidshanu b'Mitzvotav v'Tzivanu Al Netilat Lulav.

Blessed are You, Eternal, our God, Ruler of the Cosmos, The One Who has made us holy through the mitzvot and made it a mitzvah for us to take up the lulav.

On the first day only, recite the *Sheheḥeyanu.*

בָּרוּךְ אַתָּה יי אֱלֹהֵינוּ מֶלֶךְ הָעוֹלָם
שֶׁהֶחֱיָנוּ וְקִיְּמָנוּ וְהִגִּיעָנוּ לַזְּמַן הַזֶּה.

Barukh Attah Adonai Eloheinu Melekh ha-Olam she-he-Ḥeyanu, v'Kiy'manu v'Higi'anu la-Z'man ha-Zeh.

Blessed are you, Eternal, our God, Ruler of the Cosmos, Who has kept us alive, sustained us, and brought us to this season.

3. Turn the etrog over with the part that was attached to the tree facing down.

4. Shake the lulav and etrog **A** three times in front of you, **B** three times to your right, **C** three times to your left, **D** three times up, **E** three times down and **F** three times to your back.

Now shake a lulav and etrog.

REFLECTION QUESTION

What did it feel like when you shook the lulav? _____
_____.

What did you think of when you shook the lulav? _____
_____.

Check off the opportunity of shaking the etrog and lulav.

Here is a photograph of me shaking the etrog and the lulav.

Ushpizin

There is a Jewish tradition to invite famous Jews from history into the sukkah. The ushpizin list includes:

Abraham	Isaac	Jacob	Joseph	Moses	Aaron	David
Sarah	Rebekkah	Leah	Rachel	Miriam	Esther	Hannah

My List of Three Famous Jewish People

1. _____

2. _____

3. _____

My Group's List of Famous Jewish People

1. _____ 5. _____

2. _____ 6. _____

3. _____ 7. _____

4. _____ 8. _____

Check off the opportunity of Ushpizin.

Hoshanah Rabbah and Shemini Atzeret

The seventh day of Sukkot is called Hoshanah Rabbah, The Day of Great Praise. It is the last day we use the sukkah, the etrog and the lulav. We march around the synagogue with our etrog and lulav and celebrate.

The eighth day of this celebration is Shemini Atzeret, The Eighth Day of Gathering. Shemini Atzeret is the day when Jews begin praying for rain because this is the start of the rainy season in Israel.

In Reform congregations, some Reconstructionist congregations and in Israel, Shemini Atzeret and Simhat Torah are the same day. Outside of the Land of Israel, some Reconstructionist, Conservative and Orthodox Jews celebrate Simhat Torah a day later.

SIMHAT TORAH

OPPORTUNITIES

- ◯ Make a Möbius strip and compare it to the Torah.
- ◯ Write the Shema in Torah script.
- ◯ Study some Torah.
- ◯ Design a Simhat Torah flag.
- ◯ Join your class in a Torah aliyah.

FAMILY OPPORTUNITIES

- ◯ Find (or buy) and open together a family Bible.
- ◯ Attend Simhat Torah services.

SIMHAT TORAH

The Torah is like a Möbius Strip

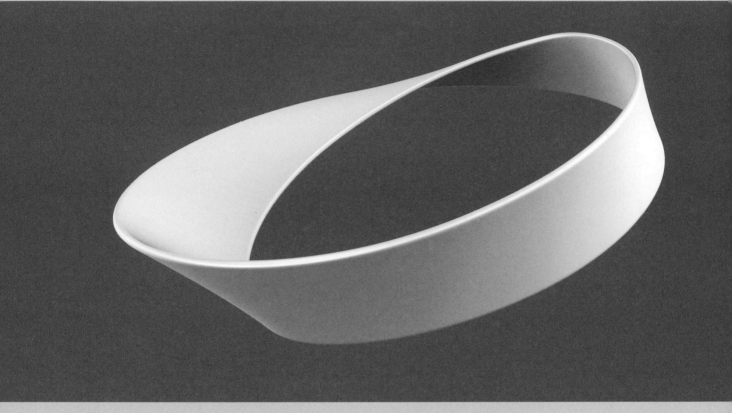

A Möbius strip has no beginning and no end. To make a Möbius strip take a long strip of paper and make a single twist. Now glue the ends together, leaving the twist. Next take a pencil or pen and draw a line down the middle. Prove to yourself that you can cover both sides and then keep going.

The Torah is like a Möbius strip. It keeps on going. It is a long strip of parchment that doesn't have a twist. The twist is in the way we read it. On the day we read the last word in the Torah, without pause we read the first words and keep going.

The day we end and begin reading the Torah is שִׂמְחַת תּוֹרָה Simḥat Torah.

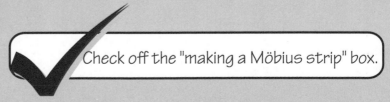

Check off the "making a Möbius strip" box.

סֵפֶר תּוֹרָה Sefer Torah

A *Simḥah* is a happy event like a bar/bat mitzvah or a wedding. The תּוֹרָה Torah is the "Five Books of Moses." It is Genesis, Exodus, Leviticus, Numbers and Deuteronomy.

In synagogue we read Torah from a סֵפֶר תּוֹרָה *Sefer Torah* (Torah scroll). The Sefer Torah is handwritten on parchment by a סוֹפֵר *sofer* (scribe). The parchment sheets are sewn together into a long scroll. The scroll is connected to wooden rollers on each side. These are called עֲצֵי־חַיִּים *Atzei Ḥayyim* (Trees of Life).

Here is the way the Shema looks in the Torah. Use a chisel-tipped pen and make a copy.

שמע ישראל יהוה אלהינו יהוה אחד

Check off the "Write the Shema" box.

33

Talmud Torah

תַּלְמוּד תּוֹרָה *Talmud Torah* (Torah study) is one of the most important Jewish things to do. We keep the Torah in the ark, but its major purpose is to be studied. Simḥat Torah is a holiday that celebrates Talmud Torah.

Jews believe that Torah is better learned with friends and that friendships are made stronger by studying together. A Torah partnership is called a *ḥevruta*, a friendship group. Pick a ḥevruta partner and study this piece of Torah.

Torah teaches us to be the kind of people that God wants us to be. The Talmud says:

> Just as God is kind, you should be kind.
> Just as God is merciful, you should be merciful.
> Just as God is holy, so should you be holy. *(Babylonian Talmud, Shabbat 113b)*

Each of you can write one addition of your own.

Name _____

Just as God is _____,

so should you be _____.

Name _____

Just as God is _____,

so should you be _____.

REFLECTION QUESTION

What is the big idea here? _____

_____

_____ .

Check off the "Study some Torah" box.

Simhat Torah

Simhat Torah is the day we celebrate the Torah. It is one of the most fun times you can have in the synagogue. We take out all of the Torah scrolls and march around the synagogue seven times. There is singing and dancing. There is much joy. Each of these Torah parades is called a *hakafah*. Everyone gets a chance to carry the Torah, touch it and dance with it. Much fun! We celebrate with the scroll as a way of making the words within it important.

דֶּגֶל *Degel* is the Hebrew word for flag. There are special Simhat Torah flags for children. The children carry and wave these flags as they march around the synagogue. The flags are part of the joy.

דֶּגֶל

Design your own Simhat Torah flag. Your flag should celebrate the Torah. It should show the celebration on Simhat Torah.

Here is a photograph of me with my Simhat Torah flag.

REFLECTION QUESTION

My flag teaches _____

_____

_____ .

Check off the "Design a Simhat Torah flag" box.

Aliyah

עֲלִיָּה *Aliyah* means "going up." It is the word used when someone moves to Israel. Aliyah is also the word used when someone is called up and given a Torah honor. On Mondays and Thursdays we read Torah, and three people are given aliyot. On Shabbat there are seven aliyot. Usually aliyot are given to adults. Bar and bat mitzvah is when a boy or girl is old enough and ready to have his or her first aliyah.

On Simḥat Torah one aliyah is given to children. It shows that even children have a connection to Torah.

My Aliyah

Here is my class having a Torah aliyah.

Mark off the "have an Torah aliyah" box.

When I looked in the Torah I thought_____

_____

_____

REFLECTION QUESTION

EREV SHABBAT

OPPORTUNITIES

◯ Give two reasons for Shabbat.

◯ Light and bless Shabbat candles.

◯ Decorate a cup and make Kiddush with it.

◯ Braid, bake and say the blessing over a <u>h</u>allah.

FAMILY OPPORTUNITIES

◯ Have a Shabbat dinner.

◯ Have a special Shabbat bedtime.

EREV SHABBAT

Erev Shabbat

At the end of the first of all days, the Torah tells us, "THERE WAS EVENING. THERE WAS MORNING, THE FIRST DAY." Ever since then, Jewish days begin at night. We begin Shabbat with the lighting of candles and the saying of the Kiddush.

Shabbat is a day of rest. On Shabbat we are supposed to be like Adam and Eve in the Garden of Eden. Our Shabbat responsibility is to enjoy the things that God created.

Two Reasons for Shabbat

One of the ways that Shabbat begins is with a blessing over the wine or grape juice. We call it the Kiddush, and it means "making holy." We use the blessing over wine as a chance to say that Shabbat is holy. In the Erev Shabbat Kiddush we are taught that Shabbat is supposed to remember two moments.

Underline the two moments in the Kiddush.

> Blessed be You, Eternal, our God,
> Ruler of the Cosmos
> Who creates the fruit of the vine.
> Blessed be You, Eternal, our God,
> Ruler of the Cosmos,
> Who made us holy through the mitzvot,
> and Who is pleased with us,
> and Who gave us the holy Shabbat
> with love and satisfaction
> as a REMEMBRANCE of the work of Creation.
> Because this is a day of Hallelujah, a holy time,
> REMEMBERING the Exodus from Egypt.
> Because You chose us and separated us
> from all other peoples
> and intentionally separated Shabbat with love
>   as our inheritance.
> Blessed be You, Eternal,
> the One Who makes Shabbat holy.

Break into groups and make up a play that shows how Shabbat is connected to these two moments.

Check off the "two reasons for Shabbat" box.

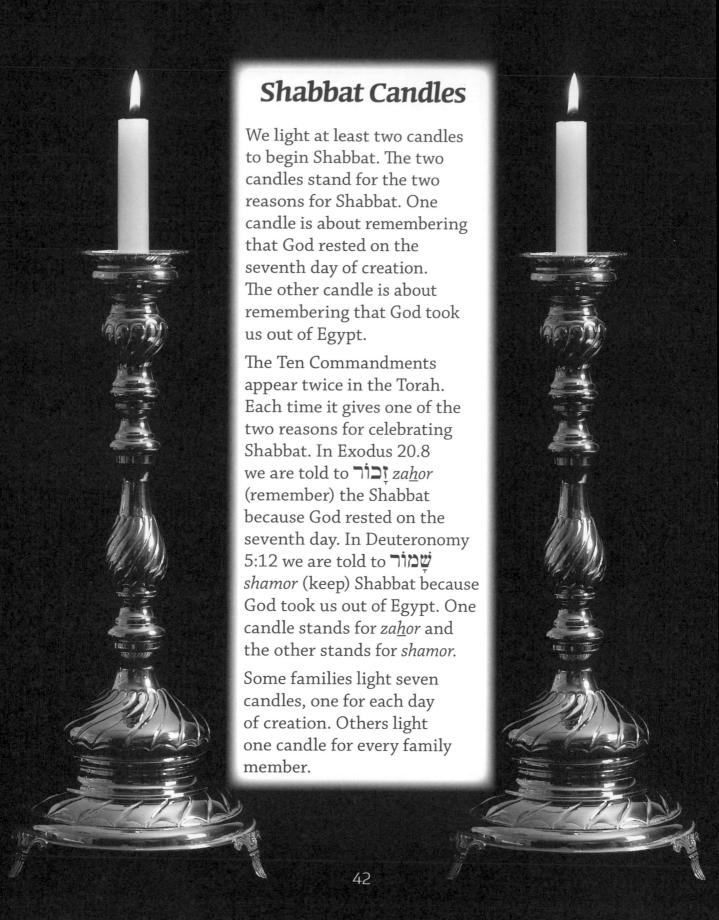

Shabbat Candles

We light at least two candles to begin Shabbat. The two candles stand for the two reasons for Shabbat. One candle is about remembering that God rested on the seventh day of creation. The other candle is about remembering that God took us out of Egypt.

The Ten Commandments appear twice in the Torah. Each time it gives one of the two reasons for celebrating Shabbat. In Exodus 20.8 we are told to זָכוֹר *zahor* (remember) the Shabbat because God rested on the seventh day. In Deuteronomy 5:12 we are told to שָׁמוֹר *shamor* (keep) Shabbat because God took us out of Egypt. One candle stands for *zahor* and the other stands for *shamor*.

Some families light seven candles, one for each day of creation. Others light one candle for every family member.

How to Light Shabbat Candles

1. Lighting Shabbat candles starts with putting money in the tzedakah box.

2. Then the candles are lit.

3. After lighting the candles we cover our eyes with our hands and recite the blessing. After the blessing some people add a silent prayer for the family.

בָּרוּךְ אַתָּה יי אֱלֹהֵינוּ מֶלֶךְ הָעוֹלָם אֲשֶׁר קִדְּשָׁנוּ בְּמִצְוֹתָיו וְצִוָּנוּ לְהַדְלִיק נֵר שֶׁל שַׁבָּת.

Barukh Attah Adonai Eloheinu, Melekh ha-Olam, Asher Kid'shanu b'Mitzvotav v'Tzivanu l'Hadlik Ner Shel Shabbat.

Blessed are You, Eternal, our God, Ruler of the Cosmos, Who made us holy with the mitzvot and made it a mitzvah for us to kindle the Sabbath light.

4. Only after the blessing is recited do we uncover our eyes and look at the lights.

Some Jews have the custom of circling the candles with their hands to make it clear that the blessing that follows connects to these candles (*Mishnah Berura 206:17*).

✓ Check off the "Light and Bless Shabbat Candles" box.

This is a photograph of me practicing the blessing over Shabbat candles.

REFLECTION QUESTION

When I look at the Shabbat candles I think of _____

_____

_____

_____

_____

Erev Shabbat Kiddush

Kiddush is another way of starting Shabbat. We use wine or grape juice as a way of thanking God for the holiness of the day. We start with the blessing for wine and then finish with a blessing for Shabbat. קָדוֹשׁ *Kadosh* means "holy." Kiddush is the way we notice and bless the holiness of Shabbat.

There are no rules about the cup used to make Kiddush, yet, Jews tend to collect beautiful cups for Kiddush. This is because of an idea called _Hiddur Mitzvah_. It means "beautifying the mitzvah." A mitzvah is an obligation from God. Jews want mitzvot to be as beautiful as possible.

The first part of the Kiddush is a blessing over wine.

בָּרוּךְ אַתָּה יי אֱלֹהֵינוּ מֶלֶךְ הָעוֹלָם
בּוֹרֵא פְּרִי הַגָּפֶן.

Barukh Attah Adonai Eloheinu Melekh ha-Olam Borei Pri ha-Gafen.

Blessed are You, Adonai, our God, Ruler of the Cosmos, Who creates the fruit of the vine.

My Kiddush Cup

Make yourself a beautiful Kiddush cup. Lots of Kiddush cups have grapes, grape vines and grape leaves, but there is no specific way your cup has to be decorated. You can do anything you want. Just make it beautiful.

Here is a photograph of me practicing Kiddush with my Kiddush cup.

Check off your "Decorate a Cup and Make Kiddush with it" box.

Making Kiddush is like _____

_____

_____

REFLECTION QUESTION

H̲allah

H̲allah is a braided loaf of egg bread that is used on Shabbat and Jewish holidays.
You need to know three things to understand h̲allah.

- It is a tradition to use two loaves of h̲allah on Shabbat. This is a memory of the double portion of manna that was collected before Shabbat. Manna was the wondrous food that fell from the sky during the forty years in the wilderness. It didn't fall on Shabbat because there was to be no work on Shabbat.

- In the Temple there was a table where twelve loaves of showbread were put out each week. The h̲allah reminds us of the showbread.

- In the Temple they took portions of the dough and offered it as a h̲allah sacrifice. Today this is only done for very large amounts of dough, not for the amount you use at home. H̲allah is a memory of the h̲allah sacrifice.

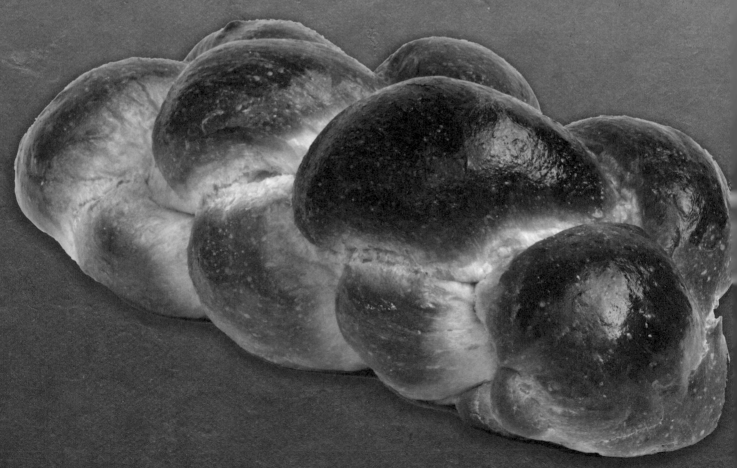

Baking Ḥallah (Makes 3–4 small ḥallot)

Ingredients
2 tablespoons dry yeast
1¾ cups warm water
½ cup sugar
⅓ cup honey
3½ teaspoons salt
½ cup oil
3 eggs plus 2 egg yolks
7 cups bread flour
1½ cups raisins or
    chocolate chips (optional)

Egg wash
2 tablespoons water
2 teaspoons sugar
1 egg plus 1 egg yolk

Directions
1. In a mixing bowl, stir together the yeast, water and a pinch of the sugar. Let the mixture stand for five minutes.
2. Stir in the remaining sugar, the honey and the salt. Add the oil, eggs, yolks and about six cups of flour and the raisins (if you are using them). Let the dough stand for 10 minutes.
3. Knead for 10 minutes, adding the remaining flour as required to make a soft and elastic dough. If the dough is still sticky, add small amounts of flour until it is soft but not sticky.
4. Let the dough rest another 10 minutes.
5. Place the dough in a greased bowl and cover with greased plastic wrap. Let the dough rise for one hour.
6. Divide the dough into 9 (for 3 ḥallot) or 12 (for 4 ḥallot) equal pieces. With each piece, form a length of dough about four inches long. Connect three pieces on one end and begin to braid the pieces together. To braid, take the piece on the right and put it over the center piece. Now take the left piece and put it over the center piece. Continue until you get to the end. Seal the ends.
7. In a small bowl, whisk together the ingredients that make up the egg wash. Brush the braided dough with the egg wash. Let the dough rise another 20–30 minutes.
8. Preheat the oven to 400°. Bake the bread for 12 minutes. Reduce the heat to 350° and bake another 25 minutes.

Over hallah we say this brakhah:

בָּרוּךְ אַתָּה יי אֱלֹהֵינוּ מֶלֶךְ הָעוֹלָם
הַמּוֹצִיא לֶחֶם מִן הָאָרֶץ.

Barukh Attah Adonai
Eloheinu Melekh ha-Olam
ha-Motzi lehem min ha-Aretz.

Blessed are You, Eternal,
our God, Ruler of the Cosmos,
Who brings forth bread from
the earth.

REFLECTION QUESTION

My hallah tastes like_____

_____

_____

_____

_____

Here is a photograph of
the hallah I made.

Check off the box that
says "braid, bake and say
the blessing over a Hallah."

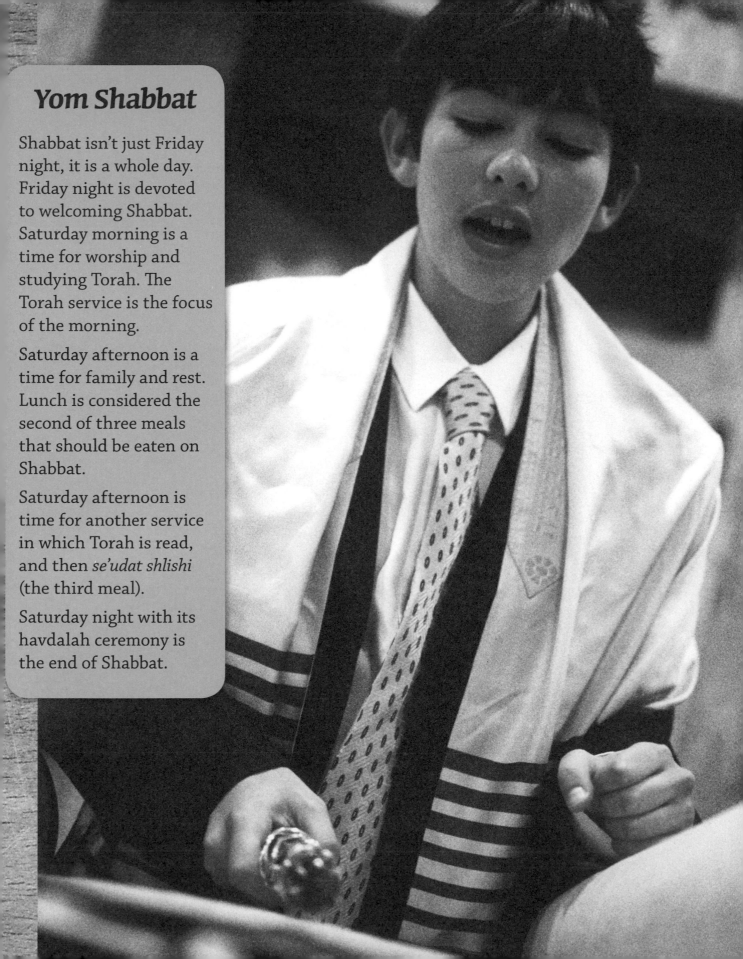

Yom Shabbat

Shabbat isn't just Friday night, it is a whole day. Friday night is devoted to welcoming Shabbat. Saturday morning is a time for worship and studying Torah. The Torah service is the focus of the morning.

Saturday afternoon is a time for family and rest. Lunch is considered the second of three meals that should be eaten on Shabbat.

Saturday afternoon is time for another service in which Torah is read, and then *se'udat shlishi* (the third meal).

Saturday night with its havdalah ceremony is the end of Shabbat.

HAVDALAH

OPPORTUNITIES

- ◯ Review and perform the *brakhah* over wine (grape juice).

- ◯ Make a container for *b'samim* and learn its *brakhah*.

- ◯ Make a Havdalah candle and learn its *brakhah*.

- ◯ Understand the concept of Havdalah.

- ◯ Participate in a Havdalah service.

FAMILY OPPORTUNITIES

- ◯ Read an Elijah story.

- ◯ Make or attend a Havdalah service.

Havdalah

On Saturday night there is a ceremony that ends Shabbat. We began Shabbat by lighting candles and blessing wine (or grape juice). At the end of Shabbat we put out a candle by dipping it in the wine. The name of this ceremony is הַבְדָּלָה *Havdalah*. Havdalah means "making a distinction." Havdalah ends Shabbat and begins the week.

We have a memory that Adam and Eve made the first Havdalah at the end of the first Shabbat. Then they left the Garden of Eden and went out into the world.

The Blessing over Wine (Grape Juice)

Most blessings are blessings over things we can see, touch, hear or smell. Sometimes Judaism wants us to say a blessing over time. There is nothing about time to see, touch, hear or smell. The Jewish tradition figured out that you could make a blessing over wine and then add a blessing over a moment.

On Saturday night, מוֹצָאֵי־שַׁבָּת Motzei Shabbat, we first say a blessing over wine. Then we add a blessing over spices, and a blessing over fire. We end with a blessing over the time of ending Shabbat.

At Havdalah it is a tradition to fill the Kiddush cup until it overflows. We lift the cup and say the "fruit of the vine" blessing.

בָּרוּךְ אַתָּה יי
אֱלֹהֵינוּ מֶלֶךְ הָעוֹלָם
בּוֹרֵא פְּרִי הַגָּפֶן.

Barukh Attah Adonai Eloheinu Melekh ha-Olam Borei Pri ha-Gafen.

Blessed are You, Eternal, our God, Ruler of the Cosmos, Who creates the fruit of the vine.

Here is a photograph of me practicing the wine brakhah.

Review and perform the brakhah over wine or grape juice.

Hit this target with a drop of wine or grape juice.

REFLECTION QUESTION

I think the Kiddush cup is filled to overflowing because _____ _____.

Spices

Spices are part of the Havdalah ceremony. We smell the spices and say a brakhah. The spices are usually kept in a box. These boxes often take the form of towers where spices could be "locked away" because they are valuable. Spices can be stored in bags or boxes, and you can even use an orange with lots of cloves stuck in it.

The blessing said over smelling the spices:

בָּרוּךְ אַתָּה יי אֱלֹהֵינוּ מֶלֶךְ הָעוֹלָם בּוֹרֵא מִינֵי בְשָׂמִים.

Barukh Attah Adonai Eloheinu Melekh ha-Olam Borei minei v'samim.

Blessed are You, Eternal, our God, Ruler of the Cosmos, the Creator of all kinds of spices.

Make your own spice container.

✔ Check off "Make a container for *b'samin* and Learn its *brakhah*."

Here is a photograph of the spice container I made.

When I smell the spices I think about _____

_____

_____

Havdalah Candle

A Havdalah candle must have at least three wicks, and it is supposed to be like a torch. A memory connects it to the torch that Adam and Eve carried as they left the Garden of Eden. That memory teaches that God taught them how to make fire so that they could make Havdalah.

The blessing over the Havdalah candle is:

בָּרוּךְ אַתָּה יי אֱלֹהֵינוּ מֶלֶךְ הָעוֹלָם בּוֹרֵא מְאוֹרֵי הָאֵשׁ.

Barukh Attah Adonai Eloheinu Melekh ha-Olam Borei m'Orei ha-Aish.

Praised are You, Eternal, our God, Ruler of the Cosmos, Who creates fire.

Make a Havdalah candle.

Check off your make a Havdalah candle box.

Drop some wax from your Havdalah candle on this target.

When I look into the flame of a Havdalah candle I think about _____

_____

_____

REFLECTION QUESTION

Holy and Ordinary

The Havdalah service is there to make distinctions. One is between Shabbat and the week. But the opportunity to divide things into holy and ordinary is the final step in the Havdalah service.

Connect the opposites that go together.

Holy   Other nations

Light   Six days of Creation

Israel   Ordinary

The seventh day   Darkness

What is the difference between a holy thing and an ordinary thing?_____

_____

Why is the end of Shabbat a good time to talk about distinctions? _____

_____

What is the difference between "Israel" and "the other nations"?_____

_____

 When you've finished this page check off "Understand the concept of Havdalah."

The Havdalah Service

Make or practice making Havdalah.

Here is the Havdalah service. We begin by lifting the cup of wine that we will not drink from until the end of the service. The first prayer speaks of redemption. Redemption is when God helps us to make the world perfect. Shabbat is like a little taste of redemption.

הִנֵּה אֵל יְשׁוּעָתִי Hineih El Y'shuati

Light the Havdalah candle. Hold up the glass of wine.

הִנֵּה אֵל יְשׁוּעָתִי אֶבְטַח וְלֹא אֶפְחָד.	*Hineih El Y'shuati, evta<u>h</u> v'Lo efhad*
כִּי עָזִּי וְזִמְרָת יָהּ יי וַיְהִי לִי לִישׁוּעָה.	*Ki ozi v'zimrah Ya Adonai, va-Y'hi Li l'Shu'ah*
וּשְׁאַבְתֶּם מַיִם בְּשָׂשׂוֹן מִמַּעַיְנֵי הַיְשׁוּעָה.	*U'shavtem mayim b'sason mi-ma'anei ha-Yishu'ah*
לַיי הַיְשׁוּעָה עַל עַמְּךָ בִרְכָתֶךָ סֶּלָה.	*l'Adonai ha-Y'shua al amkha v'ratekha selah.*
יי צְבָאוֹת עִמָּנוּ	*Adonai Tz'vot Imanu*
מִשְׂגָּב לָנוּ אֱלֹהֵי יַעֲקֹב סֶלָה.	*misgav lanu Elohei Ya'akov, selah.*
יי צְבָאוֹת אַשְׁרֵי אָדָם בּוֹטֵחַ בָּךְ.	*Adonai Tzva'ot ashrei adam bote'a<u>h</u> Bakh.*
יי הוֹשִׁיעָה הַמֶּלֶךְ יַעֲנֵנוּ בְיוֹם קָרְאֵנוּ.	*Adonai Hosiah, ha-Melekh ya'aneinu v'yom koreinu*
לַיְהוּדִים הָיְתָה אוֹרָה וְשִׂמְחָה וְשָׂשׂוֹן וִיקָר.	*la'Yihudim ha'y'tah orah v'sim<u>h</u>ah v'sasson vi'kar*
כֵּן תִּהְיֶה לָנוּ.	*Kein tih'yeh lanu,*
כּוֹס יְשׁוּעוֹת אֶשָּׂא וּבְשֵׁם יי אֶקְרָא.	*Kos Y'shuot esa uv'Shem Adonai ekra.*

Here is the God who redeems me. I am sure and unafraid,
For the Eternal is my strength and my redemption.
Joyfully you should draw water from the fountain of redemption.
The redemption belongs to the Eternal, for Your blessing to Your people, Selah.
The Eternal of Hosts is with us, the God of Israel is our safety, Selah.
The Eternal of Hosts, happy is the person who trusts in You.
Eternal save us, the Ruler who answers us when we call.
For the Jews there was light and joy, happiness and honor.
So may it be more for us. I will lift the cup of redemption and call on the Eternal.

Remain holding the cup and continue to the next blessing

The Blessing over Wine (or Grape Juice)

בָּרוּךְ אַתָּה יי אֱלֹהֵינוּ מֶלֶךְ הָעוֹלָם
בּוֹרֵא פְּרִי הַגָּפֶן.

*Barukh Attah Adonai Eloheinu Melekh ha-Olam
Borei pri ha-Gafen.*

Blessed are You, Eternal, Ruler of the Cosmos,
the Creator of the fruit of the vine.

Put the cup down. Don't drink the wine (grape juice) yet.

The Blessing over Spices

Pick up and smell the spices.

בָּרוּךְ אַתָּה יי אֱלֹהֵינוּ מֶלֶךְ הָעוֹלָם בּוֹרֵא מִינֵי בְשָׂמִים.

Barukh Attah Adonai Eloheinu Melekh ha-Olam Borei minei V'samim.

Blessed are You, Eternal, our God, Ruler of the Cosmos,
the Creator of all kinds of spices.

The Blessing over Fire

בָּרוּךְ אַתָּה יי אֱלֹהֵינוּ מֶלֶךְ הָעוֹלָם בּוֹרֵא מְאוֹרֵי הָאֵשׁ.

Barukh Attah Adonai Eloheinu Melekh ha-Olam Borei m'Orei ha-Aish.

Praised are You, Eternal, our God, Ruler of the Cosmos, Who creates fire.

Catch the light of the Havdalah candle in your fingernails.

The Blessing over Separation

בָּרוּךְ אַתָּה יי אֱלֹהֵינוּ מֶלֶךְ הָעוֹלָם   *Barukh Attah Adonai Eloheinu Melekh ha-Olam*

הַמַּבְדִּיל בֵּין קֹדֶשׁ לְחוֹל   *ha-Mavdil Bein Kodesh l'Khol*

בֵּין אוֹר לְחשֶׁךְ   *Bein Or l'Hodesh,*

בֵּין יִשְׂרָאֵל לָעַמִּים*   *bein Yisrael l'Amim,*

בֵּין יוֹם הַשְּׁבִיעִי לְשֵׁשֶׁת יְמֵי הַמַּעֲשֶׂה.   *bein Yom ha-Shvi-i l'Sheshet Y'mei ha-Ma'saseh*

בָּרוּךְ אַתָּה יי הַמַּבְדִּיל בֵּין קֹדֶשׁ לְחוֹל.   *Barukh Attah Adonai ha-Mavdil Ben Kodesh l'Khol*

Praised are You, Eternal, Ruler of the Cosmos,
the One Who separates between holy and ordinary,
between light and darkness,
between Israel and other nations,
between the seventh day and the six working days.
Praised are You, Who divides between holy and ordinary.

Now pick up and drink from the cup of wine. Then put the candle out in the wine.

Shavu'a Tov

שָׁבוּעַ טוֹב, שָׁבוּעַ טוֹב, שָׁבוּעַ טוֹב, שָׁבוּעַ טוֹב.

Shavu'a Tov, Shavu'a Tov, Shavu'a Tov, Shavu'a Tov

A good week, a week of peace, may gladness reign and joy increase.

Eliyahu ha-Navi

אֵלִיָּהוּ הַנָּבִיא, אֵלִיָּהוּ הַתִּשְׁבִּי, אֵלִיָּהוּ, אֵלִיָּהוּ, אֵלִיָּהוּ הַגִּלְעָדִי.
בִּמְהֵרָה בְיָמֵינוּ יָבוֹא אֵלֵינוּ,
עִם מָשִׁיחַ בֶּן דָּוִד, עִם מָשִׁיחַ בֶּן דָּוִד.

Eliyahu ha-Navi, Eliyahu ha-Tishabi, Eliyahu Eliyahu, Eliyahu ha-Giladi
Bimheirah b'yameinu, yavo aleinu
Im Mashiah Ben David, Im Mashiah Ben David.

Elijah the Prophet, Elijah from Tishbi, Elijah from Gilead
Come quickly to us, quickly in our day with the Messiah, the offspring of David.

 Check off the "Make or practice Havdalah" box.

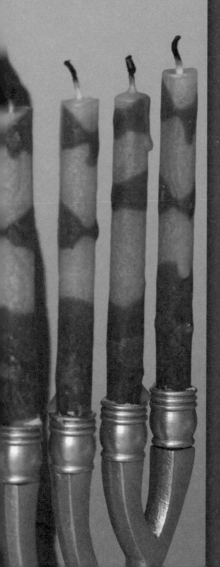

HANUKKAH

OPPORTUNITIES

◯ Participate in the story of <u>h</u>anukkah.

◯ Demonstrate lighting the <u>h</u>anukkiyah.

◯ Participate in playing and explaining dreidel.

◯ Make, eat, bless and enjoy a <u>H</u>anukkah food.

◯ Make a mezuzah and practice dedicating a Jewish home.

FAMILY OPPORTUNITIES

◯ Celebrate eight nights of <u>H</u>anukkah.

◯ Attend a <u>H</u>anukkah service.

◯ Read a Hanukkah story.

◯ Put a mezuzah on a door.

The Hanukkah Story

The Hanukkah story starts when Greeks from Syria controlled the land of Israel. They made the Jews pay taxes and had a Syrian governor.

The Greeks brought all kinds of gifts to the Jewish people. The built Greek cities with stadiums for athletics, schools to teach philosophy and temples to worship idols. Some Jews really liked this Greek stuff and made it part of the way they lived.

Other Jews wanted to keep their lives rich with Jewish living. They studied Torah, observed the mitzvot and remained loyal to the One God.

There was a lot of fighting between the Jews who liked Greek things and Jews who wanted to keep true to Judaism. Each group wanted to be in charge.

Act it Out

Act out the following:

One child in the family has a basketball game on Friday night. On the same night another child has a part in the Shabbat service. What should the family do? Then make it a single-parent family and act it out again.

REFLECTION QUESTION

How is this like the choice that Jews had to make in the time of the Greeks? _____

_____

Antiochus

The King of the Greeks in Syria was a man named Antiochus. He decided that there was too much fighting among the Jews in the Land of Israel. He said, "If they cannot decide on a religion, I will give them one." He banned everything Jewish, especially Torah teaching. He had idols of himself put all over the land and ordered all Jews to bow down to his image.

Some Jews didn't mind. Other Jews did Jewish things secretly. Some Jews already dressed like Greeks and went to the gym regularly. Other Jews studied Torah in secret and told lies about what they were doing when they gathered to have services.

Act out the following:

You live in a town with only a few Jewish families. Someone threw a cement block through the window of a Jewish home where one family had displayed their _hanukkiyah_ (_Hanukkah_ menorah). You now have a family meeting asking, "Should we display our _hanukkiyah_ tonight?"

Act it Out

How is this like the choice that Jews had to make in the time of Antiochus? _____

_____

REFLECTION QUESTION

This really happened in Billings, Montana, in 1993. That year, because of a woman named Margaret McDonald, more than 10,000 homes in Billings (almost all of them non-Jews) displayed _hanukkiyot_ in their windows.

Mattathias

The Greeks turned the Jewish Temple in Jerusalem into a garbage dump. They even brought in pigs.

Antiochus sent his soldiers from town to town testing the "Greekness" of every Jew. The soldiers had an idol and made every Jew bow down to it.

When they got to the town of Modi'in one Jew refused to bow down. His name was Mattathias. He shouted, "All who are for the One God follow me." He and his sons fled to the hills. They became the Maccabees and fought back against the Greeks.

Act out the following:

Someone in your class in school says something mean about Jews. You do nothing about it at the time, but that night you tell the story at the dinner table. Your family has a discussion about what you should do.

Act it Out

How is this like the choice that the Maccabees had to make? _____

_____

_____

REFLECTION QUESTION

Cleaning the Temple

The Maccabees won the war. The Greeks left, and the Jews went to Jerusalem to clean the Temple. The celebration of cleaning the Temple turned into an eight-day holiday that we still celebrate today. It is called Hanukkah. Hanukkah means "dedication." Hanukkah celebrates the rededication of the Temple.

We have three different memories of why Hanukkah lasts for eight days. One memory is more famous than the other two.

REFLECTION QUESTION

What lesson does each memory teach? _____

_____

_____

Which one do you believe really happened? _____

_____

_____

- The most famous memory is that when they cleaned the Temple they found only enough oil to last for one night. While they sent for new oil a miracle happened, and the oil lasted for eight nights. (Talmud, Shabbat 21b)

- The second memory is that while they were fighting, the holiday of Sukkot was missed. Sukkot was important because it was when the Jews prayed for rain. Hanukkah started as a second Sukkot. Sukkot is celebrated for eight days. (II Maccabees 10:1-8)

- The third memory is that when they cleaned the Temple they found eight iron spears. They stuck the spears in the ground, filled the ends with oil and turned the spears into the first hanukkiyah. (Pesikta Rabbati 2:1)

Check off "Participate in the story of Hanukkah."

The Hanukkiyah

The *hanukkiyah* celebrates the eight nights of Hanukkah. We add a candle every night. The purpose of the *hanukkiyah* is to advertise the miracle. That is why it is a custom to light the *hanukkiyah* in the window.

Here are the rules for lighting a *hanukkiyah*.

1. The *shamash* is the "helping candle." It is used to light the other candles. Light it first and then say all the blessings.

2. On the first night there are three blessings. On the remaining seven nights we only say the first two.

3. Always start putting the candles in from the right side of the *hanukkiyah*.

4. Always light the candles starting with the new one. This means starting the lighting from the left.

חֲנֻכִּיָּה

Fulfill the mitzvah of advertising Hanukkah by working in a small group to write and perform a Hanukkah commercial.

Hanukkiyah Blessings

#1

בָּרוּךְ אַתָּה יי אֱלֹהֵינוּ מֶלֶךְ הָעוֹלָם
אֲשֶׁר קִדְּשָׁנוּ בְּמִצְוֹתָיו
וְצִוָּנוּ לְהַדְלִיק נֵר שֶׁל חֲנֻכָּה.

Barukh Attah, Adonai, Eloheinu, Melekh ha-Olam,
Asher Kidshanu B'mitzvotav V'tzivanu l'Hadlik Ner
shel Hanukkah.

Praised are You, Eternal, our God, Ruler of the
Cosmos, Who made us holy through the mitzvot and
made it a mitzvah to kindle the Hanukkah lights.

#2

בָּרוּךְ אַתָּה יי אֱלֹהֵינוּ מֶלֶךְ הָעוֹלָם
שֶׁעָשָׂה נִסִּים לַאֲבוֹתֵינוּ
בַּיָּמִים הָהֵם בַּזְּמַן הַזֶּה.

Barukh Attah, Adonai, Eloheinu, Melekh ha-Olam,
She-asah Nissim la-Avoteinu,
Ba-Yamim ha-Hem, ba-Z'man ha-Zeh.

Praised are You, Eternal, our God, Ruler of the
Cosmos, Who made miracles for our ancestors in their
days at this very time of year.

#3

בָּרוּךְ אַתָּה יי אֱלֹהֵינוּ מֶלֶךְ הָעוֹלָם
שֶׁהֶחֱיָנוּ וְקִיְּמָנוּ וְהִגִּיעָנוּ לַזְּמַן הַזֶּה.

Barukh Attah, Adonai, Eloheinu, Melekh ha-Olam, She-
he-he'yanu, v'Kiy'manu, v'Higiyanu la-Z'man ha-Zeh.

Praised are You, Eternal, our God, Ruler of the
Cosmos, Who keeps us in life, sustains us and helps us
reach this time.

Here is a photograph of
me practicing lighting the
hanukkiyah.

REFLECTION QUESTION

When I light the hanukkiyah

I think about _____

_____

_____

_____

_____

When you've finished
practicing the Hanukkah
brakhot, check off the
"Demonstrate lighting the
hanukkiyah" box.

The Dreidel

A dreidel is a top with four sides. Each side has a letter on it. The four letters tell a story. The letters are נ *Nun*, ג *Gimmel*, ה *Hey* and ש *Shin*. The story is:

נֵס גָּדוֹל הָיָה שָׁם

Neis Gadol Hayah Sham

A great miracle happened there.

Hanukkah is the story of a miracle.
In Hebrew a dreidel is called a *sevivon*.

סְבִיבוֹן

Playing Dreidel

To know the rules for playing dreidel you need to know a little Yiddish. Yiddish is a Jewish language spoken by lots of Jews from Eastern Europe.

Everyone starts with the same pile of things. They put one in and then start taking turns spinning the dreidel. When the pot is empty, everyone puts in one again.

When the dreidel lands on נ *nun* you get *nichts*, nothing.

When the dreidel lands on ג *gimmel* you get *ganz*, everything.

When the dreidel lands on ה *hey* you get *halb*, half.

When the dreidel lands on ש *shin*, you have to *shtel*, put in.

Invent your own game that tells the Ḥanukkah story.

✔ After playing dreidel check off the "Participate in playing and explaining the dreidel" box.

Making, Eating, Blessing and Enjoying Ḥanukkah Food

Oil connects us to the Ḥanukkah story. We eat foods that remind us that "the oil lasted eight days."

The latke is a potato pancake that is fried in oil. Some people eat it with applesauce. Other people eat it with sour cream.

The blessing for a latke is:

בָּרוּךְ אַתָּה יי
אֱלֹהֵינוּ מֶלֶךְ הָעוֹלָם
בּוֹרֵא פְּרִי הָאֲדָמָה.

Barukh Attah Adonai
Eloheinu Melekh ha-Olam
Borei Pri ha-Adamah.

Praised are you Eternal, Ruler of the Cosmos, Who creates fruit of the ground.

70

Cooking Potato Latkes

Ingredients

4 potatoes, peeled and cut into quarters
1 small onion, cut into quarters
2 eggs
⅓ cup flour

1 teaspoon baking powder
¾ teaspoon salt
Freshly ground pepper
Oil for frying

Directions

1. Shred or dice the onions and potatoes. Add the eggs and mix well.
2. Add the flour, baking powder, salt and pepper and mix to make the latke batter.
3. Fill a skillet with oil until it is ¼ inch up the sides. When the oil is hot, drop in spoonfuls of the batter. Brown the latkes well on each side, turning once and pressing to flatten.
4. Drain on paper towels.
5. Serve with sour cream or applesauce.

Makes 3 to 4 dozen.

Put a drop of cold oil on this target.

Check off your "Make, eat, bless and enjoy <u>H</u>anukkah latkes" box.

Dedication

The Hebrew word חֲנֻכָּה _Hannukah_ means "dedication." The name comes from the rededication of the Temple by the Maccabees. This is when they cleaned out the Temple and rekindled the eternal light.

Jews also dedicate their homes. This ceremony is called חֲנֻכַּת הַבַּיִת _Hanukkat ha-Bayit._ בַּיִת _Bayit_ means both "house" and "family." We dedicate a Jewish home by hanging a mezuzah on the doorpost. מְזוּזָה _Mezuzah_ means "doorpost."

מְזוּזָה

REFLECTION QUESTION

When I kiss the mezuzah I think of _____

_____

_____

_____ .

Making a Mezuzah

1. A *sofer* (scribe) must write the commanded text by hand on a specially prepared *klaf* (parchment) made from a kosher animal.

2. The *klaf* must be rolled tightly, with the three paragraphs facing in and the name of God, שַׁדַּי, *Shaddai,* facing out. The rolled *klaf* is placed inside the mezuzah case.

3. Attach the mezuzah on the top third of the doorpost at a slight angle, with the top pointing inward.

4. The mezuzah should be placed on the right-hand side of the doorpost as you enter the home or room.

5. This is the blessing for attaching the mezuzah:

בָּרוּךְ אַתָּה יי אֱלֹהֵינוּ מֶלֶךְ הָעוֹלָם אֲשֶׁר קִדְּשָׁנוּ בְּמִצְוֹתָיו
וְצִוָּנוּ לִקְבּוֹעַ מְזוּזָה.

Barukh Attah Adonai Eloheinu Melekh ha-Olam Asher Kid'shanu b'Mitzvotav v'Tzivanu Lik'bo'a Mezuzah.

Blessed are You, Eternal, our God, Ruler of the Cosmos, Who makes us holy with the mitzvot and makes it a mitzvah for us to attach the mezuzah.

6. The case for a mezuzah can be bought or homemade. It can be of any size, shape or material, but it should have a שׁ *shin* or the name of God שׁדּי *Shaddai* on the face.

7. It is Jewish custom to touch the mezuzah and then kiss your fingers on leaving and entering a home. This is to remind us of that God is in the home.

8. Mezuzot can be hung on the doorposts of every room except for bathrooms.

Make your own beautiful mezuzah.

Here is a photograph of my mezuzah.

Check of the box for "making a mezuzah and practice dedicating a Jewish home."

TU B'SHVAT

OPPORTUNITIES

◯ Explain why we need trees and need Tu b'Shvat.

◯ Write a tree poem.

◯ Eat from the 7 kinds and/or 15 different fruits.

◯ Create a list of human fruits.

◯ Plant something.

FAMILY OPPORTUNITIES

◯ Plant something(s) together.

◯ Participate in a Tu b'Shvat seder.

◯ Add some habits to your family lifestyle that protect trees or the environment.

◯ Make a Power Point presentation of the story of a tree.

Tu b'Shvat

ט"וּ בִּשְׁבָט *Tu b'Shvat* is the fifteenth (ט"ו = 15) of the Hebrew month of שְׁבָט *Sh'vat*. *Tu b'Shvat* is the New Year or birthday for trees.

Torah/Mishnah: The Torah makes it important for us to know the age of trees. It teaches us when we need to share our fruit. The Rabbis knew that to know the age of a tree you need a birthday. They made Tu b'Shvat the birthday for all trees.

A **Kabbalist** is a person who works on ways to become close to God. Kabbalists believe that in a lot of ways people are like trees. When we learn about trees we learn about ourselves. They created a Tu b'Shvat seder to teach the lessons learned from trees.

The Zionists were Jews who returned to the Land of Israel and turned it into the State of Israel. They made Tu b'Shvat a time to plant trees. They used trees to turn the swamps and deserts into a lush, green, wonderful country.

Break into three groups. Have each group research one of these three questions. Share you answers.

1. Why do we need to know the age of trees?
2. How are we like trees, and what can we learn from that?
3. Why do we still need to plant trees?

My Tree

People's lives are dependent on trees. Because trees are important to the world, the Rabbis created a special blessing for those who go out in spring to see blossoming fruit trees. The blessing says: "Nothing is lacking from God's world...and God created good trees for the needs of people." (Me'Am Loez)

Go and look at a specific tree. Have your eyes follow it up and down. Look at the way the branches rise and droop. Look to see new life growing on the tree. Find the places where the tree has broken and healed. See if you can tell how it finds the light it needs. If you can, feel your tree. Get to know it. Connect to your tree, then draw as good a picture as you can of the tree you looked at.

Around the tree you drew, make a list of as many reasons as you can that we need trees.

Why We Need Trees

Work in groups to add branches to this tree.

trees conserve energy

trees give us energy

trees create places to play

trees can be a source for medicines

trees are beautiful

trees create special spaces

trees teach us things and give us a place to learn

trees can bring people together

trees limit storm damage

trees provide a place for wild animals to live

trees make the air clean

trees protect the soil

trees clean water

Check off "Explain why we need trees and need Tu b'Shvat."

A Tree Poem

"When God created Adam, God took him and showed him all the trees of the Garden of Eden and said to him, 'See my works, how beautiful they are. Everything that I created, I created it for you. Be careful not to spoil or destroy my world—for if you do, there will be nobody after you to fix it.'" *(Kohelet Rabbah 7:13)*

Write and share a tree poem.

_____

_____

_____

_____

_____

_____

REFLECTION QUESTION

What part of a tree are you? Why?_____

_____

_____

Check off "Write a tree poem".

Seven Kinds/15 Fruits and the Right Blessings

The Torah teaches us that seven kinds of fruit and grains are the most important products of the Land of Israel.

> FOR THE ETERNAL YOUR GOD IS BRINGING YOU INTO A GOOD LAND: ...A LAND OF (1) WHEAT, (2) BARLEY, (3) GRAPES, (4) FIGS AND (5) POMEGRANATES; A LAND OF OIL-YIELDING (6) OLIVES AND (7) DATE HONEY. (Deuteronomy 8:8)

The Kabbalists taught that one should eat at least fifteen fruits on Tu b'Shvat. The fifteen comes from the date, the fifteenth of Shvat.

Some people eat the seven kinds on Tu b'Shvat. Some people eat a total of fifteen nuts and fruits on Tu b'Shvat.

Do one or the other, but say the right blessing for each.

Here is the list of things I ate.

Here is a photograph of me eating seven kinds or fifteen fruits

Check off your "Eat from 7 kinds and/or 15 fruits" box.

The Right Blessings

For things that grow on trees:

בָּרוּךְ אַתָּה יי אֱלֹהֵינוּ מֶלֶךְ הָעוֹלָם בּוֹרֵא פְּרִי הָעֵץ.

Barukh Attah Adonai, Eloheinu Melekh ha-Olam, borei pri ha-etz.

Praised are You, Eternal, our God, Ruler of the Cosmos, Who created the fruit of the tree.

For things that grow in the ground:

בָּרוּךְ אַתָּה יי אֱלֹהֵינוּ מֶלֶךְ הָעוֹלָם בּוֹרֵא פְּרִי הָאֲדָמָה.

Barukh Attah Adonai, Eloheinu Melekh ha-Olam, borei pri ha-adamah.

Praised are You, Eternal, our God, Ruler of the Cosmos, Who created the fruit of the ground.

For things that grow on vines:

בָּרוּךְ אַתָּה יי אֱלֹהֵינוּ מֶלֶךְ הָעוֹלָם בּוֹרֵא פְּרִי הַגָּפֶן.

Barukh Attah Adonai, Eloheinu Melekh ha-Olam, borei pri ha-gafen.

Praised are You, Eternal, our God, Ruler of the Cosmos, Who created the fruit of the vine.

For bread:

בָּרוּךְ אַתָּה יי אֱלֹהֵינוּ מֶלֶךְ הָעוֹלָם הַמוֹצִיא לֶחֶם מִן הָאָרֶץ.

Barukh Attah Adonai, Eloheinu Melekh ha-Olam, ha-Motzi lehem min ha-aretz.

Praised are You, Eternal, our God, Ruler of the Cosmos, Who brings forth bread from the earth.

For everything else:

בָּרוּךְ אַתָּה יי אֱלֹהֵינוּ מֶלֶךְ הָעוֹלָם שֶׁהַכֹּל נִהְיֶה בִּדְבָרוֹ.

Barukh Attah Adonai, Eloheinu Melekh ha-Olam, she-ha-kol ni'h'yeh bid'varo.

Praised are You, Eternal, our God, Ruler of the Cosmos, that everything will be according to God's word.

REFLECTION QUESTION

Why do you think there are different blessings for each kind of food?

_____

_____

Human Fruits

We are taught in the Talmud and we find in the Siddur.

These are the things whose fruits a person eats in this world, but whose major reward is given in the world to come.

1. honoring father and mother,
2. deeds of loving kindness,
3. arriving early at study sessions in the morning and evening,
4. hospitality to guests,
5. visiting the sick,
6. rejoicing with the bride,
7. accompanying the dead to burial,
8. serious prayer,
9. making peace between people,
10. and the study of Torah is equal to them all (because it leads to them all).
    (Shabbat 127a)

Work in groups and brainstorm ten more things to add to this list.

1. _____
2. _____
3. _____
4. _____
5. _____

6. _____
7. _____
8. _____
9. _____
10. _____

Plant Something

Rabbi Yoḥanan ben Zakkai used to say: "If you happen to be standing with a sapling in your hand and someone says to you, 'Behold, the Messiah has come!'—first plant the tree and then go out to greet him. (Avot d'Rabbi Natan)

The most important lesson of Tu b'Shvat is to keep planting. You may have beautiful weather on Tu b'Shvat. Your entire area may be under two feet of snow. Maybe you can go outside or maybe you can't. Tu b'Shvat was originally designed for the warm weather of the Land of Israel. Now Jews celebrate it all over the world.

Plant something, somewhere, somehow.

Here is a photograph of me planting.

REFLECTION QUESTION

What did you remember when you planted? _____

_____

_____

Check off your "plant something" box.

83

OPPORTUNITIES

◯ Make a Purim mask.

◯ Examine a Megillah.

◯ Make a gragger.

◯ Act out the story of Purim.

◯ Bake hamantashen and send *Shelah Manot*.

◯ Use Purim as a tzedakah opportunity.

FAMILY OPPORTUNITIES

◯ Go to a Purim service.

◯ Send *Shelah Manot* (food gifts to friends).

◯ Give family *Matanot l'Ev'yonim* (gifts to the poor).

PURIM

Purim

Purim is the happiest day in the Jewish year. It celebrates the time when Esther defeated the wicked Haman, made Ahashuerus a better king, got her uncle Mordechai the best job in the kingdom and saved the Jewish people. Purim's story is found in the Book of Esther that we read from a handwritten scroll called a מְגִלָּה *Megillah*. We us a noisemaker called a gragger and drown out every mention of Haman.

מְגִלָּה

REFLECTION QUESTION

Do you have a best Purim memory?

What is it? _____

_____

_____

_____

Make a Purim Mask

The five big characters in the Purim Story are:

King Ahashuserus
The king of Persia who appoints Haman to be his chief advisor and who marries Esther.

Queen Vashti
The first wife of King Ahashuerus who says "no" to him, and he divorces her.

Esther
She is a Jewish woman who hides her Jewishness and who becomes Ahashuerus' next queen.

Mordechai
He is Esther's cousin, a Jewish man who would bow down only to God.

Haman
He is a wicked wicked man who is King Ahashuerus' advisor and who wants to kill the Jews.

Make a mask of one of these characters.

Here is a photograph of my Purim mask.

I picked to make a mask of _____

_____

because _____

_____

 Check off the "Make a Purim mask" box.

Unroll a Megillah

The Megillah is a handwritten by *sofer*, a scribe. Its creation follows all the same rules as a *Sefer Torah*, a Torah scroll. It is written on parchment (animal skin) using a quill (a feather turned into a pen) and a special ink. The Megillah has to be perfect. It can have no mistakes. Unlike the Torah, the Megillah is wound on only one roller.

Unroll a Megillah in your classroom. Do not touch the letters, but feel the parchment. Look at the letters. What letters or words do you know? How long is it?

REFLECTION QUESTION

What did it feel like to hold and look at the Megillah? _____

_____

_____

Check off your "unroll the Megillah" box.

Here is a photograph of my class with the Megillah.

Make a Gragger

Make a gragger, a noisemaker. In Hebrew it is called a רַעֲשָׁן *ra'ashan*. We use the gragger to make sure that Haman's name can't be heard. We make lots of noise every time Haman's name is read. Using the gragger, we prove that we are stronger than evil.

REFLECTION QUESTION

When I hear Haman's name I think about _____

_____

_____

_____ .

Check off the "Make a Gragger" box.

רַעֲשָׁן

Act Out the Story of Purim

It is a mitzvah to hear the Megillah read, but it is also a tradition to act out the story. A Purim play is called a *Purim spiel* in Yiddish.

Your class is going to produce a Purim play. You are going to use your Purim masks and your graggers. You may have extra costume pieces and props to use. Your teacher will provide you with a script. Have fun and enjoy.

Check off your "Act out the story of Purim" box.

The Four Things We Do on Purim

When Mordechai became the chief advisor to King Ahashuerus he and Esther sent a letter to all Jewish communities in the empire. It said, "Every year Jews should celebrate the fourteenth of Adar as a holiday called Purim. They should send gifts to each other and give tzedakah to the poor. They should tell the story of what happened here." From this letter come the four Purim mitzvot.

1. Hearing the Megillah

2. Celebrating

3. Sending *Shelah Manot*—gifts of food to friends.

4. Giving *Matanot l'Ev'yonim*—gifts to the poor.

Bake Hamantashen and Send Shela<u>h</u> Manot

Hamantashen are Purim cookies named after Haman. They are made in the shape of triangles. One opinion about the triangles is that Haman had a hat shaped like a triangle. The other opinion is that Haman's ears were shaped like triangles.

We call the gifts of food that we give to friends and family *Shela<u>h</u> Manot*. The basic rule is that you must include at least two different kinds of food. You are to give these gifts to your friends (and family). There are no rules about whom to include.

Hamantashen

Ingredients

2 tablespoons vegetable shortening

2 tablespoons butter

⅓ cup sugar

1 egg

1 tablespoon orange juice

½ teaspoon vanilla

1⅓ cups flour

pinch of salt

egg wash made of egg and water

pie filling, jam or preserves, chocolate chips

Directions

1. Preheat the oven to 350°. Grease baking sheets.

2. Cream together the shortening and sugar. Add the egg and blend until smooth. Stir in the orange juice and vanilla.

3. Fold in the flour, salt and baking powder and mix to make a firm but soft dough. Cover and let rest ten minutes. Divide dough and work with one portion at a time.

5. Roll out dough on lightly floured board to a thickness of ¼ inch. Use a 3-inch cookie cutter and cut into rounds. Brush rounds with egg wash.

6. Using a spoon, fill the rounds with the filling. Draw three sides together by folding two sides toward the center to form the top and the remaining dough toward the center to meet the other edges. Brush with egg wash.

7. Bake until golden brown, about 18-20 minutes. When done, remove hamantashen from cookie sheet to cool. Makes 3 to 4 dozen.

Make up a package for *Shelah Manot*. Deliver it to a friend or family member.

In this circle tape some crumbs from your hamantashen.

Check off your "Bake Hamantashen and send Shelah Manot" box.

Giving Matanot l'Eviyonim

Mordechai and Esther made it a mitzvah for us not only to give gifts to our friends but to make sure that we take care of the poor at the same time. This mitzvah is called *Matanot l'Ev'yonim*. Purim is about celebration. Celebration must include those in need, too.

Your class is going to decide on a tzedakah project that is worthy of receiving your gift. Your job is to do research (probably on the internet) and bring in information on one possibility. You may want to ask your parents for suggestions.

Name: _____

Basic mission: _____

_____

Things they do: _____

_____

_____

Work out a classroom process to have everyone share tzedakah choices and narrow them down to one.

As a class we decided to give our *Matanot l'Ev'yonim* money to:

_____

_____

_____

because they do good work helping to

_____

_____

_____

_____

Here is a photograph of my class allocating our Matanot l'Ev'yonim.

 Check off your "Matanot l'Ev'yonim" box.

PASSOVER

OPPORTUNITIES

- ⃝ Ask and answer the Four Questions.
- ⃝ Bake and eat matzah.
- ⃝ Make and eat haroset.
- ⃝ Tell your own story of being a slave in Egypt.
- ⃝ Make and eat maror in a Hillel sandwich.
- ⃝ Say the plagues and dip out grape juice with your finger.
- ⃝ Sing Dayyenu.

FAMILY OPPORTUNITIES

- ⃝ Create, modify or supplement your family Haggadah.
- ⃝ Have or attend a seder.
- ⃝ As a family, keep Passover for the week.

Slaves in Egypt

Jacob and his family moved to Egypt. The Torah tells us that Egypt had a new Pharaoh who turned the Jews into slaves. We spent four hundred years in slavery doing hard work and having a bitter life. Eventually God brought us out of Egypt. On our last night in Egypt we had a seder. A seder is a special meal combined with a service that is done family by family. Every year on that same night we still have a seder.

When you were a slave in Egypt, what was your job?_____

_____

_____

The Four Questions

Perhaps the biggest responsibility you have at the seder is asking the four questions. Now is the time to make sure that you are good at it. Practice the four questions.

מַה נִּשְׁתַּנָּה הַלַּיְלָה הַזֶּה מִכָּל הַלֵּילוֹת?

Mah nishtanah ha-lailah ha-zeh mi-kol ha-leilot?

Why do we make this night very different from all other nights?

שֶׁבְּכָל הַלֵּילוֹת אָנוּ אוֹכְלִין חָמֵץ וּמַצָּה הַלַּיְלָה הַזֶּה כֻּלּוֹ מַצָּה?

She-b'kol ha-leilot anu okhlin ḥametz u'matzah, ha-lailah ha-zeh kulo matzah?

On all other nights we can eat either hametz or matzah—
why on this night can we eat only matzah?

שֶׁבְּכָל הַלֵּילוֹת אָנוּ אוֹכְלִין שְׁאָר יְרָקוֹת הַלַּיְלָה הַזֶּה מָרוֹר?

She-b'kol ha-leilot anu okhlin she'ar yirakot, ha-lailah ha-zeh kulo maror?

On all other nights we eat all kinds of vegetables—
why on this night must we eat bitter herbs?

שֶׁבְּכָל הַלֵּילוֹת אֵין אָנוּ מַטְבִּילִין אֲפִילוּ פַּעַם אֶחָת הַלַּיְלָה הַזֶּה שְׁתֵּי פְעָמִים?

She-b'kol ha-leilot ein anu matbilin afilu pa'am eḥat, ha-lailah ha-zeh s'tei f'amim?

On all other nights we do not dip vegetables even once—
why on this night do we dip them twice?

שֶׁבְּכָל הַלֵּילוֹת אָנוּ אוֹכְלִין בֵּין יוֹשְׁבִין וּבֵין מְסֻבִּין הַלַּיְלָה הַזֶּה כֻּלָּנוּ מְסֻבִּין?

She-b'kol ha-leilot anu okhlin bein yoshvin u'vein m'subin, ha-lailah ha-zeh kulanu misubin?

On all other nights we can eat either sitting up or resting on our side—
why on this night do we eat resting on our side?

The Four Answers

The Haggadah, the book that "orders" our seder, gives us questions but no answers.

You have already practiced the questions. Now get together with a group of two or three other students and work on answers for those questions.

1. On all other nights we can eat either _hametz_ or _matzah_—
   why on this night can we eat only matzah?

   _____

   _____

   _____

2. On all other nights we eat all kinds of vegetables—
   why on this night must we eat bitter herbs?

   _____

   _____

   _____

3. On all other nights we do not dip vegetables even once—
   why on this night do we dip them twice?

   _____

   _____

   _____

4. On all other nights we can eat either sitting up or resting on our side—
   why on this night do we eat resting on our side?

   _____

   _____

   _____

Share your answers with the class.

✓ Check off your "Ask and answer the Four Questions" box.

The Lessons of Matzah

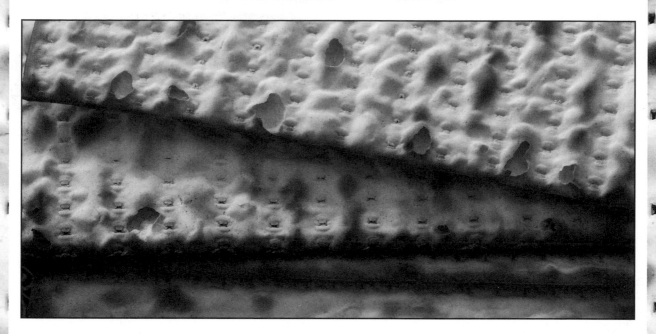

We are taught three different things about matzah.

- Matzah was the bread baked that did not have time to rise as we Jews fled from Egypt.
- Matzah was the poor bread that was all we had to eat when we were slaves in Egypt.
- Matzah is the bread of freedom. It becomes the taste of our liberation.

Matzah is just bread and water. It doesn't rise. _Hametz_ is the opposite of matzah. It is any food that is not kosher (acceptable) for Pesa<u>h</u>. Matzah is basic. _Hametz_ is anything that has risen, that has become thicker.

Some things to talk about first with a partner, then with the whole class.

1. How does the bread of slavery turn into the bread of freedom?
2. What is one part of you that is matzah (basic)?
3. What is one part of you that is _hametz_ (swelled)?

מַצָּה

Making Matzah

Ingredients

2 cups all-purpose flour
1 cup whole-wheat flour
   water

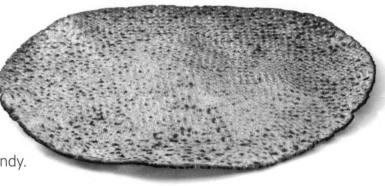

NOTE: You only have 18 minutes from the time the flour meets the water to put the matzah in the oven, or the dough will begin to rise. Have a timer handy.

Instructions

1. Preheat the oven to 450–500 degrees (or higher), or use the broiler. Use a cookie sheet covered with foil or parchment paper.
2. In a large bowl, mix 2 cups all-purpose flour and 1 cup whole-wheat flour and water until you have a soft, kneadable dough.
3. Knead for about 5 minutes.
3. Let the dough rest for a couple of minutes.
4. Break off egg-sized portions of dough and stretch each portion as thin as you can. Then roll it into even thinner oval slabs.
6. Prick each slab with a fork.
7. Place slabs on the baking sheets, and as soon as a sheet is filled, place it in the oven.
8. Bake until matzah is crisp and buckled, about 3 minutes. Cool.

Check off the "Make and eat matzah" box.

Tape Matzah crumbs on this circle.

The <u>H</u>aroset Story

<u>H</u>aroset is a mixture of fruit, nuts and wine (grape juice) that represents the mortar that Jewish slaves used to hold the bricks together. In the seder we dip the *maror*, the bitter herb in <u>h</u>aroset. Many Jews add it to the "Hillel sandwich" that is made up of matzah and maror.

There are many different <u>h</u>aroset recipes from all over the world. Almost every Jewish community has one. Look on the internet and find one you like. (Hint: Try "Charoset.")

The <u>h</u>aroset recipe that interests me comes from: _____

The <u>h</u>aroset we made in class comes from: _____

Here is a really basic <u>h</u>aroset recipe.

Ashkenazic <u>H</u>aroset

Ingredients
    3 medium apples
    ½ cup chopped walnuts (optional)
    1 teaspoon honey
    ½ teaspoon cinnamon
    1½ tablespoons sugar
    3 tablespoons red wine or grape juice

Instructions
1. Peel, core and chop or grate the apples into moderately coarse pieces.
2. In a bowl, toss the apples with the walnuts, honey, cinnamon and sugar.
3. Stir in the 3 tablespoons grape juice. Keep in the refrigerator until it is served—at least one hour.

Check off the "Make and eat <u>h</u>aroset" box.

For We Were Slaves...

> In each generation every person should feel as though he or she had actually gone out from Egypt. (The Haggadah)

In the Haggadah this prayer is the answer to the four questions. Read it. Explain it. Then tell your own story of being a slave in Egypt.

We were slaves to Pharaoh in Egypt, and the Eternal, our God, took us from there with a mighty hand and with an outstretched arm.

If the Holy One Who is to be praised had not taken our families out of Egypt, then we, and our children, and our children's children would still be slaves to Pharaoh in Egypt.

Now, even if all of us were scholars, even if all of us were elders, even if all of us were well-learned in the Torah, it would still be a mitzvah for us to tell the story of the Exodus from Egypt.

The more we tell the story of the Exodus, the more we deserve to be honored.

My Exodus

On Pesa<u>h</u> we learn how to feel like the Jews who were slaves in Egypt. Tell your own story of what it was like to be a slave. Next act out a conversation between slaves.

When I was a slave in Egypt, my job was _____ .

The one thing I hated most about being a slave was _____

_____ .

Even though it was horrible being a slave, the one thing that kept me going was _____

_____ .

The one thing being a slave taught me was_____

_____

Check off your "tell your own story of being a slave in Egypt" box.

Making Maror

מָרוֹר

Maror is the bitter herb. It is usually horseradish. We eat it during the seder to remember the bitterness of slavery in Egypt. The Torah tells us that the Egyptians "made their lives bitter with hard slavery, in mortar and in brick, and in all manner of work in the field…" (Exodus 1:14)

Horseradish root is not that hot when you simply cut into it. It becomes much more bitter when you grate or grind it.

REFLECTION QUESTION

What was the most bitter thing that happened to you when you were a slave in Egypt? _____

_____

_____

What is a bitter thing in your life? ___

_____

_____

Here are some directions for how to create your own hot horseradish.

Maror

Ingredients
1 cup peeled and cubed horseradish root
¾ cup white vinegar
2 teaspoons sugar
¼ teaspoon salt

Directions
Place all ingredients in a blender or food processor and pulse until desired consistency.

Make a Hillel sandwich with matzah, maror and haroset. Hillel was ancient rabbi who used to eat maror this way.

Check off "Make and eat maror in a Hillel sandwich" box.

105

The Plagues

God begins to bring Israel out of Egypt with ten plagues. When we read them, we stick our little finger in the wine (or grape juice) and take a drop of wine out of our glass. We make our joy smaller because of the bad things that had to happen.

צְפַרְדֵּעַ

frogs   t'fardei'a

דָּם

blood   dam

שְׁחִין

s'hin
boils

דֶּבֶר

dever
cattle
disease

עָרֹב

arov
insects

kinim
lice

כִּנִּים

מַכַּת בְּכוֹרוֹת

makat b'khorot
death of the firstborn

חֹשֶׁךְ

darkness   hoshekh

אַרְבֶּה

locust   arbeh

בָּרָד

barad
hail

Repeat the plagues after your leader and hit this target with your drops of grape juice.

Check off the "Say the plagues and dip out grape juice with your finger" box.

Dayyenu

One of the ways we thank God for everything God has done for us is by singing *Dayyenu*. *Dayyenu* means "It would have been enough."

God has given us many gifts:

אִלּוּ הוֹצִיאָנוּ מִמִּצְרַיִם. דַּיֵּנוּ.

Ilu hotzi'anu mi-mitzrayim—dayyenu.
Had God only taken us out of Egypt: *Dayyenu.*

אִלּוּ נָתַן לָנוּ אֶת הַשַּׁבָּת. דַּיֵּנוּ.

Ilu natan lanu et ha-shabbat—dayyenu
Had God only given us Shabbat: *Dayyenu.*

אִלּוּ נָתַן לָנוּ אֶת הַתּוֹרָה. דַּיֵּנוּ.

Ilu natan lanu et ha-Torah—dayyenu.
Had God only given us the Torah: *Dayyenu.*

אִלּוּ הִכְנִיסָנוּ לְאֶרֶץ יִשְׂרָאֵל. דַּיֵּנוּ.

Ilu hikh'ni'sanu l'Eretz Yisrael—dayyenu
Had God only led us to the land of Israel: *Dayyenu.*

Create your own *Dayyenu* verse:

Had God only _____

_____. *Dayyenu.*

Check off the
"Sing Dayyenu" box.

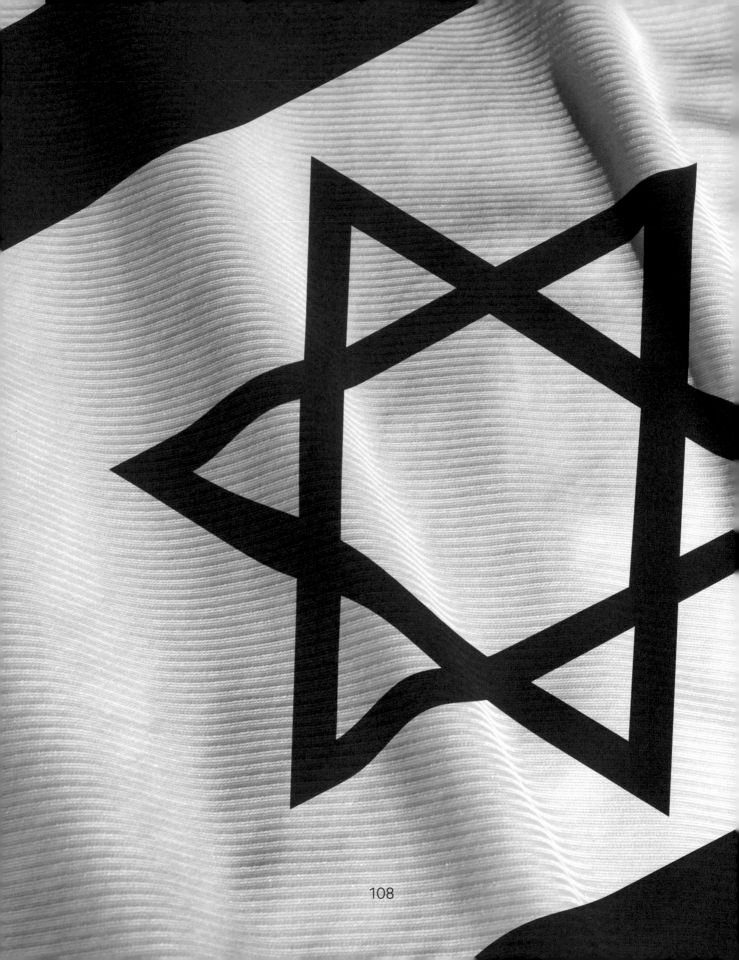

OPPORTUNITIES

◯ Observe a moment of silence and then sing *Ha-Tikvah*.

◯ Fill in locations on a map of Israel.

◯ Learn an Israeli dance.

◯ Go on an internet Israeli shopping trip.

◯ Make and eat an Israeli snack.

FAMILY OPPORTUNITIES

◯ Attend a community Israel event.

◯ Make real (or imaginary) plans for a family trip to Israel.

◯ Have an Israel birthday party.

YOM HA-ATZMA'UT

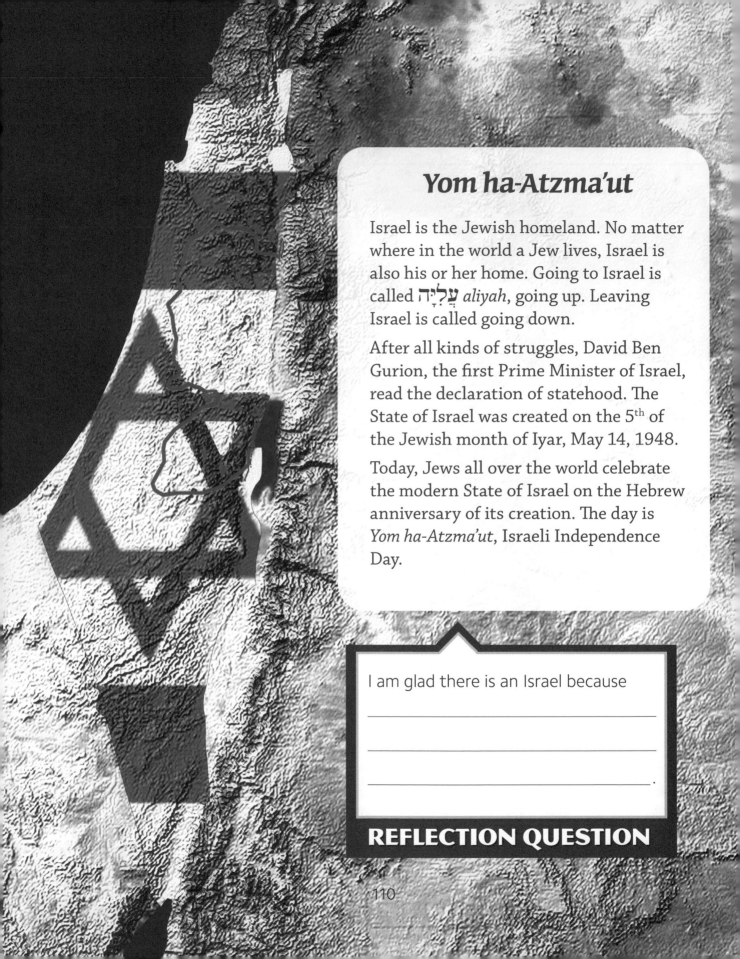

Yom ha-Atzma'ut

Israel is the Jewish homeland. No matter where in the world a Jew lives, Israel is also his or her home. Going to Israel is called עֲלִיָּה *aliyah*, going up. Leaving Israel is called going down.

After all kinds of struggles, David Ben Gurion, the first Prime Minister of Israel, read the declaration of statehood. The State of Israel was created on the 5th of the Jewish month of Iyar, May 14, 1948.

Today, Jews all over the world celebrate the modern State of Israel on the Hebrew anniversary of its creation. The day is *Yom ha-Atzma'ut*, Israeli Independence Day.

I am glad there is an Israel because

_____

_____

_____.

REFLECTION QUESTION

Yom ha-Zikaron

On the day before Yom ha-Atzma'ut Israel celebrates *Yom ha-Zikaron*, the Day of Remembrance. This is a memorial day for all those who died to keep the Jewish State alive and free. At 11.00 A.M. on Yom ha-Zikaron a siren blows, and all of Israel comes to a stop. There are two minutes of silence to remember those who have given their lives.

הַתִּקְוָה
Ha-Tikvah

The national anthem of Israel is called *Ha-Tikvah*, the Hope. Naphtali Herz Imber wrote a poem called *Tikvatenu*, "Our Hope". Samuel Cohen loved the poem and matched part of it to a folk tune called "Cart and Oxen." Together they became the national anthem of Israel, *Ha-Tikvah*.

On the next page is a text for *Ha-Tikvah*. Once you've learned how to sing it, observe a moment of silence and then sing it again.

Ha-Tikvah

כָּל עוֹד בַּלֵּבָב פְּנִימָה נֶפֶשׁ יְהוּדִי הוֹמִיָּה.
וּלְפַאֲתֵי מִזְרָח קָדִימָה עַיִן לְצִיּוֹן צוֹפִיָּה.

עוֹד לֹא אָבְדָה תִּקְוָתֵנוּ. הַתִּקְוָה בַּת שְׁנוֹת אַלְפַּיִם.
לִהְיוֹת עַם חָפְשִׁי בְּאַרְצֵנוּ אֶרֶץ צִיּוֹן וִירוּשָׁלָיִם.

Kol od ba-levav p'nimah nefesh yehudi homiyah.
u'lfatei mizrah kadimah, ayin l'tziyon tzofiyah.

Od lo avdah tikvateinu ha-tikvah bat sh'not alphayim.
lih'yot am hofshi b'artzeinu eretz tziyon vi'rushalayim.

As long as in the heart, within, a Jewish soul still yearns,
And onward toward the East, an eye still watches toward Zion—

Our hope has not yet been lost, the two-thousand-year-old hope,
To be a free nation in our own homeland, the land of Zion and Jerusalem.

My hope for Israel is: _____

_____

_____

_____ .

REFLECTION QUESTION

✓ Check off "observe a moment of silence and then sing *Ha-Tikvah*."

The Land of Israel

Israel is a small country, about the size of the state of New Jersey, but it's got all kinds of different geography. You can find a mountain with snow and a beach with coral. You can find big cities, cities built on the sides of hills, cities in deserts and the lowest point on earth. Knowing the land is one way of knowing Israel.

Put the following places on you map of Israel.

Jerusalem   Mediterranean Sea
Tel Aviv   Dead Sea
Haifa   Galilee
Eilat   Jordan River
Negev   Kinneret (Sea of Galilee)

REFLECTION QUESTION

When I go to Israel the thing I most want to see in Israel is:

_____

_____

_____ .

✓ Check off the "fill in locations on a map of Israel" box.

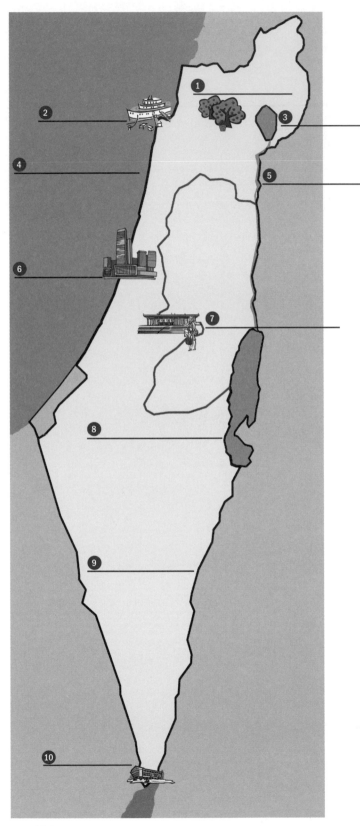

114

Singers, Dancers, Artist, Writers and Poets

David Broza performing at sunrise concert in Masada (2007)

Israel is a place for Jewish culture. It is a country of singers, writers and poets. There are lots of filmmakers, actors and dancers. Israelis design fashion and high tech, create crafts and turn the desert green. Israel is a place of creation. It is a center of medical innovations, of new software breakthroughs, and it is doing a great job turning sea water into fresh water. In Israel something is always going on.

With your parents' or teachers' help you can listen to Israeli music, look at some Israeli art, watch some Israeli films and discover some of this creativity.

To celebrate Israel's creativity, learn a new Israeli dance.

Check off "learn an Israeli dance."

Internet Shopping Trip

Using a computer at home (with your parent's help) or at school (with your teacher's help), find a place where you can pick out and buy one of each of the following that you like.

An Israeli T-shirt _____

An Israeli painting_____

A piece of Israeli jewelry _____

Candlesticks created by an Israeli artist _____

An Israeli book _____

One other thing I want is _____

I found it at _____

 Check off "go on an internet Israeli shopping trip".

Israeli Food

Jews have come to Israel from over eighty countries. They have brought with them Jewish versions of local foods.

There are two basic categories of food in Israel. *Ashkenazic* food is food that came primarily from Eastern Europe, such as Poland, Russia and Germany. *Sefardic* food came from Northern Africa, Turkey and Southern Europe. So in Israel you find both schnitzel (a breaded and fried piece of chicken) and *shakshuka* (a dish that starts with poached eggs cooked in a sauce of tomatoes, peppers, onions and spices and is served with pita bread). It is a country of matzah balls and falafel balls.

Israeli Recipes

Pita Chips

Ingredients

6 pita bread pockets
¼ cup olive oil
¼ teaspoon ground black pepper
½ teaspoon garlic salt
¼ teaspoon dried rosemary

Directions

1. Preheat oven to 400 degrees.

2. Cut each pita into 8 triangles. Place triangles on a cookie sheet covered in parchment paper.

3. In a bowl, combine the oil, pepper, salt and rosemary. Brush the triangles with the oil mixture.

4. Bake in the preheated oven for about seven minutes, or until lightly browned and crispy.

Hummus

Ingredients

1 can of garbanzo beans
¼ cup tahina (sesame paste)
½ cup lemon juice
3 cloves garlic, finely chopped
1 teaspoon salt
1 teaspoon pepper
3 tablespoons extra-virgin olive oil

Directions

1. Pour all the ingredients into a big bowl.

2. Using your hands (or a potato masher), mush all the ingredients together until it feels kind of like peanut butter.

3. Use a spatula to put the hummus on a plate or in a small bowl. Drizzle some olive oil on top. (Israelis like to decorate their hummus with paprika or toasted pine nuts.)

My favorite Israeli food is_____

_____

_____ .

REFLECTION QUESTION

Check off the "Make and eat an Israeli snack" box.

SHAVUOT

OPPORTUNITIES

- ◯ Count the days from Pesa<u>h</u> to Shavuot.
- ◯ Make a storyboard of the *Bikkurim* prayer.
- ◯ Make your classroom green.
- ◯ Tell a personal story of Mt. Sinai.
- ◯ Participate in a midnight Torah study.
- ◯ Act out the Book of Ruth.

FAMILY OPPORTUNITIES

- ◯ Make a *milkhig* meal for Shavuot.
- ◯ Go to a confirmation or Shavuot service.
- ◯ Green your house for Shavuot.

Weeks

Work in groups of 3-4. Your teacher will give you a few pages from this year's Jewish calendar.

1. Count the number of days from the second day of Passover to Shavuot.

   _____

2. How many weeks are involved? _____

   _____

3. Why would the Jewish name of this holiday be called שָׁבוּעוֹת *Shavuot*, weeks?

   _____

   _____

✔ Check off the "Count the days from *Pesaḥ* to Shavuot" box.

Shavuot

Shavuot is the day we remember Moses getting the Torah on the top of Mt. Sinai.

Shavuot is the feast of weeks. It is one of the three pilgrimage festivals. A pilgrimage festival was when Jews in ancient Israel went up to Jerusalem to celebrate. Sukkot and Pesah were pilgrimage festivals that each lasted a week. Shavuot is the only pilgrimage festival that is only a day (or two).

There is a tradition to count the omer. This is a prayer for each of the forty-nine days between the second day of Passover and the day before Shavuot. These seven weeks are the time of harvesting grain. It starts with the barley harvest and ends with the wheat harvest.

Shavuot is also *Hag ha-Bikkurim*, the Festival of the First Fruits. Shavuot was the first time that new fruit could be brought to the Temple.

Bikkurim

Jewish farmers used to tie a reed around the first of each kind of species to grow. Just before Shavuot they would cut fruits and put them in silver and gold baskets. The baskets would be loaded on oxen whose horns were decorated and whose bodies were covered in flowers. These oxen were marched through the country and up to Jerusalem, up to the Temple. When the farmers came to present their fruit they said five biblical verses that tell the story of the Jewish people.

A wandering Aramean was my father.
He went down into Egypt and lived there
He started out as a family that were few in number.
He became there a nation, great, mighty and populous.

And the Egyptians treated us badly, and were cruel to us, and made us do hard slavery.

And we cried out to the ETERNAL, the God of our fathers, and the ETERNAL heard our voice,
and saw our bad treatment, and our work, and our slavery.

The ETERNAL brought us out of Egypt
with a mighty hand and an outstretched arm,
with great terror, with signs and wonders.

And God brought us into this place, and gave us this land, a land flowing with milk and honey. (Deuteronomy 26:5-10)

Work in groups of five to make a storyboard of this biblical prayer. A storyboard is a set of pictures that tell the order of shots in a movie.

Check off your "make a storyboard of the Bikkurim prayer" box.

Make Your Classroom Green

We remember that when the Families-of-Israel came to Mount Sinai it burst into life with flowers and greenery. It was no longer desert. From this memory it has been a Jewish custom practiced by many communities to decorate synagogues and homes with flowers and other greens. The places that are really serious about decorating for Shavuot are kibbutzim in Israel. They really understand a harvest holiday.

Decorate your classroom for Shavuot. Make it a team effort. Assign different groups to make different things. Use your storyboards as part of the decorations.

Check off the "Make your classroom green" box.

Here is a photograph of our green classroom.

When I Was at Mount Sinai

The Midrash teaches (Exodus Rabbah 28.5) that every Jew who ever lived and who ever will live was at Mt. Sinai. When you were standing, waiting for the Torah, whom did you see? To whom did you talk?

Name a famous Jew whom you saw at Sinai: _____

_____

Think of a question you would like to ask your famous Jew. _____

_____

Imagine how the Jew you chose to meet at Sinai would answer that question:

_____

_____

Imagine going from Egypt to Mount Sinai. Imagine hearing God teach Torah. You are going to share your memories of what that was like. Your teacher is going to ask you a series of questions to help you remember.

 Check off your "personal story of Mt. Sinai" box.

Midnight Torah Study

We remember that on the morning that B'nai Yisrael were to receive the Torah, the people overslept. God was waiting on top of Mount Sinai, and Moses had to wake up *B'nai Yisrael*. To make sure that they would never miss another giving of the Torah, Jews began the tradition of studying all night on Erev Shavuot.

You are not going to study all night, but ask your parents to wake you up at midnight on *Erev Shavuot* to study this Torah together.

ABRAM MEETS GOD

When Abraham was a boy he was called "Abram." This is a story about Abram. This is not a Torah story. It is a midrash. It is a story that grows out of a Torah story.

Long ago Nimrod was a wicked king. Nimrod wanted everyone to bow to him. Nimrod wanted everyone to treat him like a god. Nimrod wanted everyone to believe that he was a god.

One night a huge star came into the sky and ate four other stars. It ate the North Star. It ate the South Star. It ate the East Star. It ate the West Star.

Nimrod asked his wizards, "What does this mean?"

The wizards all said, "A boy has been born who will let people know that you are only a person."

Nimrod said two things. Nimrod first said, "I am a god." Then Nimrod said, "Kill the boy."

For three years they searched for the child. Tera_h_ and Amtela were scared. They hid their son Abram in a cave. They wanted him to be safe.

Abram stayed in the cave day and night and looked out at the world. He was lonely. He was scared. He wondered, "Who created the world?" He wondered, "Why am I here?"

Abram saw the sun. The sun was hot. The sun gave light. The sun gave life. Abram thought, "The sun must be god." Then a wind blew a cloud in front of the sun. It got darker. Abram said, "The wind can stop the sun. The wind must be god."

Night came. When the sun went down, the wind stopped. Then the moon rose. Abram said, "The moon must be god." He thought about her all night long.

In the morning, the sun rose again. Abram knew that the sun could not be god. Then Abram suddenly knew the truth. He said, "There must be one God who created everything. One God made the sun. The same God made the wind. The same God made the moon. The same God made Nimrod. And the same God made me. I believe in one God."

Then Abram heard a voice that said, "I am here, My son. I believe in you."

Abram said, "I am not alone anymore. I am not afraid anymore." Then Abram began to pray.

Check off the "midnight Torah study" box.

REFLECTION QUESTION

1. How can God whom we cannot see be more powerful than the sun, the moon and stars that we can see?

   _____

   _____

2. What do you think Abram said in his prayer? _____

   _____

   _____

Here is a photograph of our midnight study session.

The Book of Ruth

1. Long ago there was a famine in Israel. Elimelekh, his wife Naomi and their sons Ma<u>h</u>lon and <u>H</u>ilion moved to Moab. Both sons find wives in Moab. Then Naomi's husband and her two sons die.

2. Naomi decided to return to Israel. She told her daughters-in-law to return to their own mothers and remarry. Orpah left, but Ruth said, "DON'T ASK ME TO LEAVE YOU, OR TO STOP FOLLOWING YOU; FOR WHERE YOU GO, I WILL GO; AND WHERE YOU LIVE, I WILL LIVE; YOUR PEOPLE WILL BE MY PEOPLE, AND YOUR GOD, MY GOD." (Ruth 1:16)

3. Naomi and Ruth returned to Bethlehem. It was harvest time. To support her mother-in-law and herself, Ruth went to the fields to glean. Gleaning is picking up the stocks of grain that are dropped or left behind. Ruth went to a field belonging to a man named Boaz. Boaz was good to her. Ruth told Naomi of Boaz's kindness.

4. It turned out that Boaz was a close relative of Naomi's husband's family. Naomi sent Ruth to the threshing floor at night. Boaz awoke, and Ruth reminded him that he had a family obligation to save Ruth and Naomi. Boaz said he was willing to marry Ruth but informed Ruth that there was another male relative who had the right of first refusal.

5. The next morning Boaz talked over the problem with the other male relative before the town elders. The other male relative gave Boaz permission. Boaz and Ruth married.

Break into five groups. Have each group take one of the scenes to act out.
Do it with puppets. Perform the story.

REFLECTION QUESTION

The book of Ruth reminds me of the story of _____

_____

_____.

 Check off "act out the book of Ruth" box.